The Muslim Guide
to Wellbeing

by the same author

Working Within Diversity
A Reflective Guide to Anti-Oppressive Practice in Counselling and Therapy
Myira Khan
ISBN 978 1 83997 098 6
eISBN 978 1 83997 099 3

of related interest

The Mixed + Multiracial Guide To Wellbeing
Navigating Family, Identity + Healing
Namalee Bolle
ISBN 978 1 80501 365 5
eISBN 978 1 80501 366 2

Your Worry Makes Sense
Anxiety and Burnout are Logical (and You Can Overcome Them)
Dr Martin Brunet
Illustrations by Hannah Robinson
ISBN 978 1 80501 297 9
eISBN 978 1 80501 298 6

Burnout-Free Working
Your Expert Guide to Thriving in a Stressful Workplace
Dr Richard Duggins
ISBN 978 1 80501 246 7
eISBN 978 1 80501 247 4
Audio ISBN 978 1 39982 876 5

The Ultimate Anxiety Toolkit
25 Tools to Worry Less, Relax More, and Boost Your Self-Esteem
Risa Williams
Illustrated by Jennifer Whitney and Amanda Way
ISBN 978 1 78775 770 7
eISBN 978 1 78775 771 4

The Ultimate Self-Esteem Toolkit
25 Tools to Boost Confidence, Achieve Goals, and Find Happiness
Risa Williams
Illustrated by Jennifer Whitney
ISBN 978 1 83997 474 8
eISBN 978 1 83997 475 5

The Ultimate Time Management Toolkit
25 Productivity Tools for Adults with ADHD and Chronically Busy People
Risa Williams
Illustrated by Jennifer Whitney
ISBN 978 1 83997 178 5
eISBN 978 1 83997 179 2

The Muslim Guide to Wellbeing

A Faith-Sensitive Guide to Nurturing Personal, Spiritual and Relationship Growth

Myira Khan

Foreword by Tahirah Yasin

Jessica Kingsley Publishers
London and Philadelphia

First published in Great Britain in 2026 by Jessica Kingsley Publishers
An imprint of John Murray Press

1

Copyright © Myira Khan 2026

The right of Myira Khan to be identified as the Author of the Work has been asserted
by her in accordance with the Copyright, Designs and Patents Act 1988.

Foreword copyright © Tahirah Yasin 2026

Front cover image source: Shutterstock®.

A CIP catalogue record for this title is available from the
British Library and the Library of Congress

ISBN 978 1 80501 347 1
eISBN 978 1 80501 348 8

Printed and bound by CPI Group (UK) Ltd, Croydon, CR0 4YY

Jessica Kingsley Publishers' policy is to use papers that are natural, renewable and recyclable
products and made from wood grown in sustainable forests. The logging and manufacturing
processes are expected to conform to the environmental regulations of the country of origin.

Jessica Kingsley Publishers
Carmelite House
50 Victoria Embankment
London EC4Y 0DZ

www.jkp.com

John Murray Press
Part of Hodder & Stoughton Ltd
An Hachette Company

The authorised representative in the EEA is Hachette Ireland, 8 Castlecourt Centre,
Dublin 15, D15 XTP3, Ireland (email: info@hbgi.ie)

'O Allah, bless this work with barakah and make it a source of goodness and guidance for all who benefit from it. Grant us sincerity in our intentions and success in our efforts. Ameen.'

To my support circle.
For your duas and support, I am in deep gratitude.

Contents

Introduction

Section One: Relationship with Allah (swt)

Section Two: Relationship with Self

Section Three: Relationship with Others

Tools and Resources

Foreword

With profound admiration, reverence, and great honour, I introduce Myira Khan's latest work – a groundbreaking, practical, and faith-sensitive guide to wellbeing. This book is another self-help guide and a Muslim's comprehensive personal, spiritual, and relationship growth manual. Written with a deep understanding of the unique needs of the Muslim community, Myira's work offers a vital resource for individuals seeking balance and fulfilment in their lives, grounded in Islamic teachings and contemporary psychological principles.

I first came across Myira Khan's name over a decade ago, during my early days as a trainee in a predominantly white, middle-class area of Gloucestershire. At the time, I was searching for a Muslim therapist – someone who could understand and address the intersection of my cultural and religious identity in a therapeutic setting. When I discovered Myira's work through *Therapy Today*, I was beyond thrilled. She was like a beacon of light in what had often felt like a lonely and isolating journey. To me, Myira was not just a therapist; she was a role model, a pioneer, and a celebrity in the therapy field. She had carved out a space where Muslim communities could access culturally competent mental health resources. In this space, the stigma around mental health could be dismantled with compassion, empathy, and understanding.

Myira's career is nothing short of remarkable. From founding the first Muslim counselling therapy directory to being a vocal advocate for culturally competent therapy, she has made unparalleled contributions to the mental health field. Her tireless work has created a bridge for Muslim individuals to seek the support they need while also encouraging therapists to adopt a culturally sensitive and holistic approach to their practice.

In her TED talk, 'Grow to Glow: The Art of Flowfilment', Myira introduced the concept of 'flowfilment' – thriving, living a life that seamlessly integrates genuine self-care and fulfilment. She challenged conventional notions of self-care and encouraged people to delve deeper. Curiosity, individuals, thriving...

Witnessing her articulate these insights on such a prominent platform was profoundly inspiring, as it was the first time I saw someone from our background addressing these vital topics in such a public forum. And her presence at conferences discussing mental health, diversity, and the intersection of culture and therapy has paved the way for crucial conversations about how we can better support Muslim clients and those from other marginalized communities.

This book is a natural extension of Myira's mission to support Muslims in navigating their wellbeing through a lens that is deeply rooted in faith. Myira saw a gap in the resources available to the Muslim community – a gap that needed to be filled with a guide combining practical psychological tools and spiritual insights. This book addresses that gap beautifully by offering a unique blend of cognitive behavioural therapy (CBT) exercises, self-reflection activities, and spiritual guidance, all written in a manner that is accessible, jargon-free, and deeply aligned.

The book's structure is purposely designed to help readers take meaningful steps towards healing and personal growth. It begins with an exploration of the relationship with the self – our nafs – and then moves into how we interact with others. Through simple but powerful reflections and exercises, Myira helps readers identify unhelpful thought patterns, navigate emotional challenges, and cultivate a deeper connection with themselves and those around them. Each exercise is a practical tool that can be easily implemented daily, offering real-world solutions to complex emotional and spiritual issues.

This book's unwavering commitment to faith and cultural relevance sets it apart. While many therapeutic resources can feel disconnected from one's spiritual identity, Myira's work is grounded in the understanding that true wellbeing cannot be achieved without considering one's relationship with Allah, faith, and the cultural context that shapes one's experience. The book acknowledges that spirituality is central to healing, particularly within the Muslim community. It integrates these elements with the principles of CBT to provide a genuinely holistic approach.

Myira's entrepreneurial spirit is evident throughout this work. Her commitment to making therapy and wellbeing accessible to Muslims in a way that is both meaningful and respectful of their religious values shines through every page. This is the first-ever guide of its kind, offering a practical approach to mental health and personal growth while honouring the teachings of Islam. The exercises and worksheets provided in the book are not merely theoretical; they are practical, actionable steps designed to help readers understand their mental health and actively work towards improving it.

This book invites readers to reflect, grow, and heal for the sake of their faith. Myira's vision is clear – to provide a spiritually enriching and practically transformative resource, helping Muslims navigate the complexities of modern life while staying connected to their faith and values. The simple, achievable exercises help readers cultivate a more profound self-awareness, build healthier relationships, and foster a greater connection with Allah.

As a psychotherapist, I have long recognized the importance of offering clients culturally sensitive and spiritually aligned resources. Myira's work, including this book, is a testament to the fact that mental health care cannot be one-size-fits-all – it must be personalized and rooted in individuals' lived experiences. This book is a gift to many, offering wisdom and guidance.

I am truly honoured to write this foreword for a book that will undoubtedly serve as a beacon of light for countless Muslims looking to enhance their mental, emotional, and spiritual wellbeing. I pray that Allah grants this book success and barakah, and that it becomes a source of healing, empowerment, and growth for all who read it. Undoubtedly, Myira's work will continue to inspire and uplift individuals, offering them the tools they need to build a life of balance, peace, and connection – with themselves, others, and, most importantly, Allah.

Tahirah Yasin
Psychotherapist/Clinical Supervisor
CEO of Neurodirectory

Introduction

Welcome to *The Muslim Guide to Wellbeing*

If you've picked up *The Muslim Guide to Wellbeing*, you're likely someone looking for practical, faith-sensitive and culturally sensitive tools to support your wellbeing, emotional health and sense of self (or to support your Muslim clients, if you are a therapist, counsellor, coach or practitioner who supports Muslim clients and communities).

This book is for you if you're seeking a balanced, accessible approach to self-care and wellbeing that aligns with your faith and identity as a Muslim yet doesn't require theological expertise or heavy psychological jargon. Whether you're curious about self-care and wellbeing considered from a Muslim perspective or framework, or a seasoned wellness seeker, this book aims to offer something meaningful, practical and easy to integrate into your daily life.

Why this book?

As a counsellor and coach with over 16 years of experience working with Muslim clients, I've come to see common challenges and needs for culturally and faith-sensitive approaches to therapy, mental health, wellbeing and self-care. In therapy and coaching sessions, I often explore topics with my clients such as self-compassion, boundaries, healthy relationships and how to find calm and peace amidst life's demands. These are universal aspects of wellbeing, but what I also hear repeatedly is the need for tools and guidance that don't ignore cultural, faith or personal identities. Muslims who want to engage in wellbeing and self-care practices often ask for guidance that respects their values, connects with their identity, faith and beliefs, and supports their spiritual and emotional growth in ways that feel natural, accessible and contextualized within their faith and belief system.

A unique approach to wellbeing and self-care

Unlike many wellness guides, this book addresses wellbeing and self-care through faith-based and anti-oppressive lenses, relevant to Muslims in a world where they may face unique societal pressures. Here, you'll find guidance on how to support your own wellbeing while honouring the complexities of your identity. This book is practical and reflective, designed as a how-to guide that anyone can pick up and implement. It offers a wide range of practical and emotionally reflective tools for building healthier relationships with yourself, with others and with Allah (swt). It is a guide for those who want to nurture their wellbeing in ways that honour both their values and their unique experiences. The strategies and reflections here invite you to see yourself as worthy – to meet your needs, to grow, to find contentment and to look after yourself with love, kindness and compassion. It blends culturally sensitive practices with anti-oppressive approaches, recognizing the importance of wellbeing and self-care frameworks that respect and honour Muslims navigating complex identities and contexts.

Why listen to me?

I am a Muslim counsellor and coach of over 16 years' experience, specializing in anti-oppressive, faith-appropriate and culturally sensitive approaches and practices to emotional, mental and psychological health and wellbeing. My experience and expertise in this field allow me to deeply understand the nuanced ways that faith, identity and sense of self intersect with wellbeing and health. I've written this book to bridge gaps I've noticed in resources for Muslims, aiming to provide an accessible, faith-sensitive and culturally rooted, compassionate path to self-care and spiritual, emotional, mental and psychological health and wellbeing.

How to use this book

Consider *The Muslim Guide to Wellbeing* an emergent, ongoing process of discovery. While this book uses a faith-sensitive context, it is not a book on Islamic psychology, nor is it a theological or scholarly text. Rather, it's a practical guide to wellbeing and self-care, written by a Muslim counsellor and coach, with a focus on everyday, meaningful actions that you can integrate into your life to foster optimal wellbeing for yourself, from within an Islamic frame. It is a book for anyone looking to cultivate a sense of balance and wellbeing that is deeply rooted in respect for their faith, identity and individual needs. This book can be used before, during and after any journey in therapy or coaching.

There is space to respond within the book, but you can also download larger, full-page copies of any material marked with ✦ from www.jkp.com/catalogue/book/9781805013471 to use in your daily wellbeing practice. You may also want to use your own notebook for additional reflections and responses to the material.

Please note throughout the book, where Allah (swt) is written, 'swt' stands for 'Subhanahu Wa Ta'ala', meaning 'Glorified and Exalted is He', which is used as a mark of reverence for Allah (swt). Where 'SAW' is mentioned in any Quran translation, 'SAW' stands for 'Sallallahu Alayhi Wasallam'. It is mentioned after the name of the Prophet Muhammad (SAW), and translates as 'Peace and blessings be upon him'.

For all Quran verses, the English translations have been referenced from *Translation of the Meanings of the Holy Quran into the English Language* by Hilali and Khan (1997).

What to expect

Throughout this guide, you will find reflections, exercises and key themes on topics such as self-compassion. self-esteem and self-love, emotions, emotional needs and emotional regulation and boundaries, relationship blueprints and healthy relationships. My hope is that each chapter will offer you simple, achievable tools for building and maintaining your optimal wellbeing, as well as deeper insights into how you can support yourself on the journey. This book is an invitation to nurture your wellbeing from a place of self-respect, compassion and acceptance.

The Muslim Guide to Wellbeing is here to serve as your companion in this journey – a path to a balanced, faith-aligned approach to wellbeing and self-care.

All good in this book is from Allah (swt). All mistakes and shortcomings are mine.

Introduction

CHAPTER 1

Wellbeing

What is wellbeing?

Wellbeing is a concept that varies across cultures and faiths, reflecting their values, beliefs, worldviews and sense of self. Across all definitions, there are some commonalities that wellbeing encompasses and these include the care and looking after of emotional, physical, mental and social health.

However, the various cultural definitions of wellbeing each emphasize, prioritize and focus on certain aspects of health based on their belief and value systems. This ranges from a Western perspective which focuses on individual self-care, prioritizing autonomy, achievement and personal pleasure and happiness, through to Indigenous and traditional perspectives, Eastern faith and philosophies, African and Latin American perspectives and more contemporary global perspectives, which bring anti-oppressive, spiritual, environmental, ancestorial, collectivist, community and social dimensions into focus alongside physical, mental and emotional health.

An Islamic understanding of wellbeing

An Islamic understanding of wellbeing is a holistic approach, encompassing spiritual, emotional, mental, physical, social and professional components. Islamic wellbeing is focused on bringing about balance in a person's heart, soul and character, through submission to Allah (swt) and fulfilling their responsibilities and obligations to Allah (swt), oneself and others. Islamic wellbeing is rooted and modelled in the teachings of the faith.

The key components of wellbeing are:

- spiritual wellbeing – spiritual connection and fulfilment
- emotional wellbeing – emotional regulation and balance
- mental wellbeing – mental clarity
- social wellbeing – healthy relationships and meaningful connections
- physical wellbeing – good physical health

- professional and financial wellbeing – aligned career and financial values.

The key components of wellbeing are met and reflected through a holistic self-care practice, which is described in Chapter 3.

Islamic wellbeing strives for harmony, balance and success in both this world (dunya) and in the Hereafter (Akhirah), by cultivating a life that aligns with your faith and its guidance and teachings, through your intentional relationships with Allah (swt), yourself, others and the world around you.

A faith-sensitive approach to wellbeing for Muslims is inherently an anti-oppressive approach, as it takes a collective view of wellbeing and self-care, and resists the individualistic, capitalist, commodified view of wellbeing and self-care. It rejects wellbeing and self-care as luxury, external or shallow action, and instead reclaims wellbeing and self-care as necessary, deserving and a duty upon you, in your everyday life, and for a healthy sense of self and identity and relationships, including for your spiritual self.

Optimal wellbeing derives from both individual self-care action, focus and benefits and from collective community-centred, social action, activities, connections and relationships. It celebrates wellbeing as a practice inherent in your faith beliefs and values that manifests in your everyday relationships with yourself, with others and with Allah (swt).

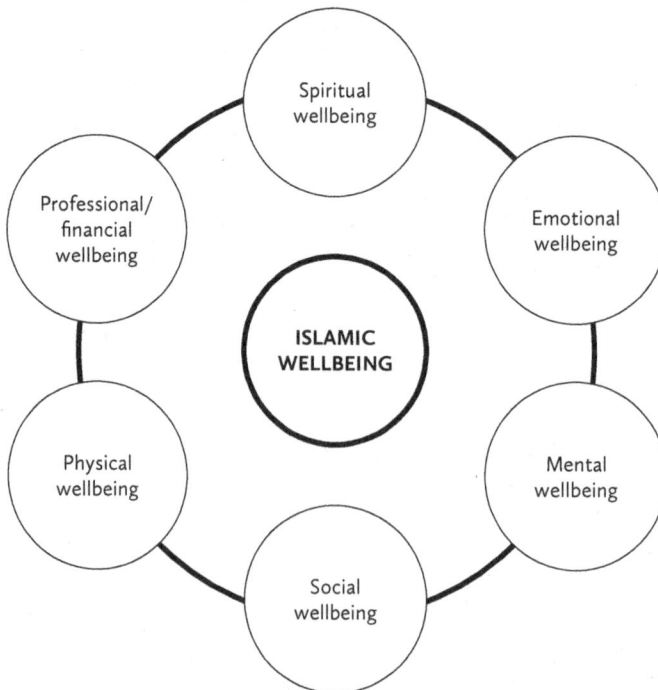

Key components of wellbeing in Islam

Wellbeing is a journey

There is no end point or finish line when it comes to your wellbeing. It is a process and journey. The experience of wellbeing comes from the practice of it, not its completion. The continual process and journey is one of reconnecting to yourself, to others and to Allah (swt) for your optimal wellbeing.

Wellbeing is an invitation to yourself. To discover what makes you feel fulfilled, well and balanced. To commit to your journey of wellbeing, as an act of self-love, self-compassion and duty of care, to look after yourself and your relationships, which align with your faith beliefs and values.

Healing (shifa) and health include spiritual, emotional and mental components alongside physical health. Healing is from Allah (swt), as the ultimate source of healing, while your effort, intention and commitment to supporting your own health and wellbeing, and seeking guidance and implementing healthy practices are also advocated.

You deserve to feel good about yourself and fulfilled in your everyday life. The tools, techniques and practices in this book support you in your efforts and intentions for optimal wellbeing.

REFLECTIONS

What are your feelings, thoughts and reflections from this chapter? What are you sitting with?

. . . .

. . . .

. . . .

What is your current practice or relationship with your overall wellbeing and with different components of your wellbeing?

. . . .

. . . .

. . . .

Using the following wellbeing wheel, rate your current level of satisfaction for each component of wellbeing, on a scale of 0 (low) to 10 (high).

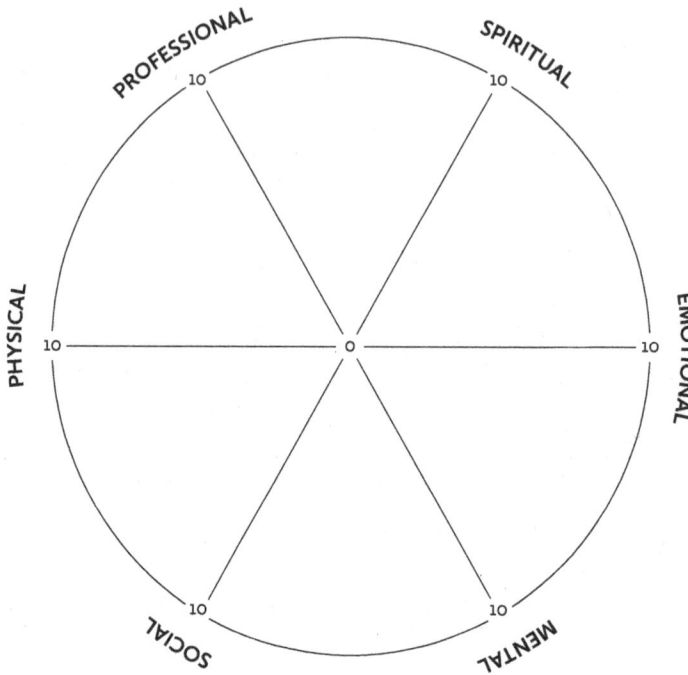

Wellbeing wheel

You can use this wellbeing wheel template anytime to reassess your wellbeing satisfaction ratings and to identify areas for attention.

Reflecting on your ratings, what feelings or thoughts do you have? Does any rating surprise you? Are there ratings that are higher or lower than you expected?

. . . .

. . . .

. . . .

What are the gaps in your wellbeing and which components of wellbeing need attention? (See Chapter 16: Self-Growth to identify areas and goals for improvement.)

. . . .

. . . .

. . . .

Use the tools, techniques and practices in this book to support all components of your wellbeing.

CHAPTER 2

Model of Wellbeing for Muslims

A model of wellbeing for Muslims is comprised of three interrelated dimensions, these being your relationship with Allah (swt), relationship with self and relationship with others, which offers a holistic approach that blends spirituality, personal growth and social connection. This three-dimensional model fosters a balanced, nurtured and flourishing life, supporting and nurturing your spiritual, emotional, mental, physical, social and professional wellbeing.

Wellbeing model: the three dimensions

The three dimensions each represent one of the three relationships:

1. relationship with Allah (swt)
2. relationship with self
3. relationship with others.

Collectively, this represents a model for holistic and integrated wellbeing, which is the balance and harmony that comes from nurturing all three relationships. Each of the relationships supports and strengthens the other two, reflecting the interdependence between spirituality, self-care and community. When one relationship is neglected, it can affect the balance and harmony of the holistic and integrated structure.

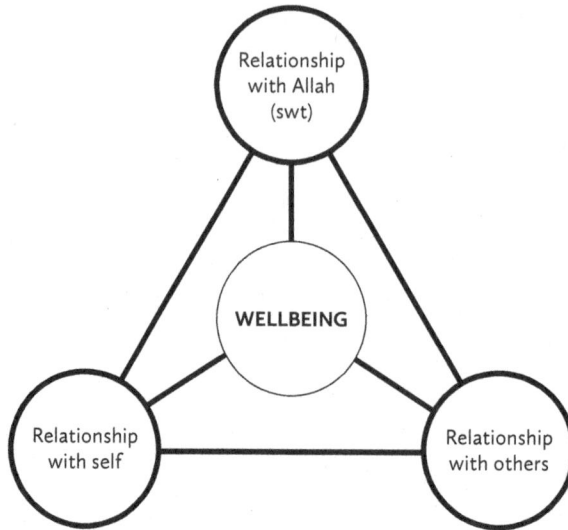

Model of wellbeing for Muslims

Relationship with Allah (swt)

Cultivating a meaningful relationship with Allah (swt) supports your wellbeing, primarily your spiritual wellbeing. Nurturing a deep and fulfilling connection with the Creator brings meaning and purpose, inner peace, a sense of calm, centredness and moral clarity to your life. It involves faith, trust and reliance on His divine guidance, as well as practices that strengthen and deepen this relationship.

This relationship is central to a Muslim's spiritual health and wellbeing, as it aligns your thoughts, emotions and actions with the principles of Islam and supports you to establish and maintain a deep connection and relationship with Allah (swt), which manifests in every aspect of your life, lived experience and sense of self. Your relationship with Allah (swt) is at the heart of your wellbeing.

There are many principles and practices to foster your relationship with Allah (swt) for spiritual health and holistic wellbeing. Further details on these principles and practices are discussed in Chapter 5: Relationship with Allah (swt).

Relationship with self

Cultivating a meaningful relationship with yourself supports your wellbeing and all its components. This dimension refers to nurturing a deep connection to yourself through increased self-awareness, self-care, self-love, self-compassion and personal growth and development. Cultivating a relationship with yourself fosters a deep-seated self-relationship of love, compassion and self-acceptance towards a strong, robust and anchored sense of self and identity, which honours and respects your lived experience and 'truth'.

Practices to foster this relationship with yourself and connection for wellbeing include:

- **Self-awareness and self-reflection:** Regularly checking in with yourself and your emotional, physical, mental and spiritual states to identify where your needs are being met and where they are not, and what you can do to support yourself to feel content and fulfilled.

- **Self-compassion and self-acceptance:** Consistently and unconditionally offering yourself kindness, compassion, non-judgement and acceptance, to all parts and aspects of yourself.

- **Physical needs:** Practising physical health through provision of a healthy lifestyle via healthy nutrition, regular exercise, quality sleep and accessing any medical care or treatment if required.

- **Growth and self-development:** Identifying and working towards personal goals, acknowledging successes and achievements, and engaging in any self-development activities, to support your wellbeing and overall lifestyle.

- **Emotional regulation and balance:** Acknowledging, processing and navigating through emotions and engaging in emotional regulation and emotionally supportive tools and activities to balance, contain and nurture emotions for an optimal wellbeing state.

Further details on these practices are discussed in the chapters in Section Two: Relationship with Self.

Relationship with others

Cultivating meaningful relationships with others – your family, friends, wider social circles and broader communities – supports your wellbeing, with a particular emphasis on your social wellbeing. This dimension refers to nurturing a deep connection to others through fostering healthy relationships, a sense of belonging, engaging in a community, sharing common values and beliefs, respecting social responsibility and offering collective and mutual support.

Principles and practices to foster this connection for social wellbeing include:

- **Empathy:** Practising actively listening to others and supporting others' feelings and needs.

- **Compassion:** Offering to support others and meeting their needs, especially during times of difficulty or challenge.

- **Communication:** Practising clear and open communication skills to support honest and understood conversations and relationships.

- **Mutual support and responsibility:** Engaging in the mutual support of meeting one another's needs, where support and responsibility are equally shared, with a communal responsibility towards the duty of care of each other and wider social and community circles.

- **Boundaries:** Establishing and maintaining boundaries to foster healthy relationships, which support and protect your optimal wellbeing.

- **Conflict resolution:** Resolving conflicts constructively, problem solving, being solution-focused and working collectively on issues and concerns from a unified position.

Further details on these practices are discussed in the chapters in Section Three: Relationships with Others.

Model interconnections: how these relationships support wellbeing

Each dimension of the model is interconnected and influences the others:

1. **Relationship with Allah (swt) and self:** A strong spiritual connection fosters self-awareness, self-worth and self-compassion, allowing individuals to view and accept themselves as a valued creation of Allah (swt), belonging to Allah (swt) and being given rights, duties and responsibilities to look after themselves and their wellbeing.

2. **Relationship with Allah (swt) and others:** As faith emphasizes love, kindness and service to others, this encourages the intention to cultivate

and maintain healthy relationships. It supports everyone to treat one another with respect, care and compassion.

3. **Relationship with self and others:** Cultivating a healthy relationship with yourself mirrors and influences the healthy relationships you look to have with others. Showing compassion, love and respect to yourself communicates the same values that you can offer to others. As you learn to build better boundaries, meet your needs and hold and honour your emotions in your relationship with yourself, you increase your ability to build better boundaries, communication and empathy with others, leading to overall healthier relationships, which in turn support your wellbeing.

The model of wellbeing is not about individual self-care and wellbeing practices which are conducted in isolation, but is an integrated approach that arises from the interconnected three dimensions and relationships, leading to a complete and whole sense of wellbeing, which contributes towards a fulfilled, content and peaceful sense of self.

REFLECTIONS

What are your reflections from this chapter?

. . . .

. . . .

. . . .

What is your current experience of these three relationship dimensions?

. . . .

. . . .

. . . .

How might you now consider them in your wellbeing? What can you do to further support your three relationship dimensions?

. . . .

. . . .

. . . .

1. Relationship with Allah (swt):

. . . .

. . . .

2. Relationship with self:

. . . .

. . . .

3. Relationship with others:

. . . .

. . . .

CHAPTER 3

Self-Care

What is self-care?

Let me start by saying what self-care is not. Self-care is not selfish. Self-care is not automatically an expensive or indulgent activity. Self-care is not doing something just because you feel you 'should', when it doesn't bring any purpose or fulfilment to your wellbeing. Self-care is not doing something that can be defined as self-care so it looks good to everyone else on the outside but doesn't bring you joy and happiness.

Self-care is the opposite of these things.

Self-care is the practice to improve, maintain and support your wellbeing. It is the 'how-to' practical means to look after your spiritual, emotional, mental, social, physical and professional wellbeing needs and components in your life.

Self-care is more than just an occasional day-off, time to yourself, indulgent bubble bath or day at the spa. Self-care is an intentional and consistent practice in how you show up, prioritize and take responsibility to meet your needs and look after yourself in your daily life through your actions, behaviours, thoughts, decisions and relationships. It is not an afterthought, but an integrated and embedded part of your daily lifestyle. A consistent, intentional and integrated self-care plan of everyday habits and routines is the most effective and sustainable. Your regular and habitual self-care habits help to support and nurture your wellbeing, to foster your growth, purpose and fulfilment in life.

Self-care is an awareness of balance. Of the energy you pour into yourself and what you pour out of yourself into your relationships, work, family, commitments, duties and daily life. Finding balance, through nurturing your wellbeing and self-care, can be conceptualized as the 'art of flowfilment' – the flow and fulfilment of energy in and out of you – which became the topic of my TED talk in early 2020.

The 'art of flowfilment' invites you to intentionally reflect and identify what heathy self-care practices you are choosing to engage in, to allow nurturing, soothing, replenishing, fulfilling energy to flow into you, and how you manage that energy, your boundaries and relationship with self, for energy to healthily and appropriately pour into, nurture and replenish your life and your relationships with others, which in turn benefits your wellbeing.

So, self-care is not a one-size-fits-all plan. It is bespoke and customized to your needs and how you can best optimize your daily lifestyle, routine and habits to support your wellbeing and find balance. However, the central foundations and pillars within Islam, which directly meet some of your wellbeing and self-care needs, such as prayer, form a core and common part of a self-care plan for all Muslims.

Your self-care and wellbeing plan will be unique to you, and it will be what works for you. It may not work for others. You may feel this when you are given advice or a suggestion for a self-care activity, but it just doesn't resonate with you or support you to feel good about yourself. Discovering your self-care and wellbeing plan is personal to you, as it needs to work for you. Listen to what you need and honour that. Being flexible with your self-care plan is also important. Perhaps what you need from one day to the next will differ, but over time this will change too. What once felt good for you may no longer feel as supportive, restorative or nourishing to you. So listen and keep attuned to yourself and what you and your body are telling you about what you need and what feels good.

Key components of wellbeing

The key components of wellbeing are met and reflected through a holistic self-care practice. Let's look at each wellbeing component and the self-care practices that support it.

Spiritual self-care is a dimension of wellbeing that relates to your sense of purpose, meaning, and connection to Allah (swt). Spiritual self-care centres on nurturing the soul. It focuses on your relationship with Allah (swt) and how to strengthen your connection with Him through practices such as prayer (salah), supplication (dua), fasting, intentions (niyyat), patience (sabr) and gratitude (shukr). Further details and examples can be found in Chapter 4: Self-Care Planning and Chapter 5: Relationship with Allah (swt).

Emotional self-care supports the dimension of emotional wellbeing that relates to practices which help you foster emotional regulation and awareness, process and manage emotional distress or dysregulation, and nurture emotional balance and robustness. Practices for emotional self-care involve fostering a relationship with yourself, including setting healthy boundaries, processing emotions, practising emotional regulation techniques and raising self-awareness. Further information on these practices can be found in Section Two: Relationship with Self.

Mental self-care supports the dimension of mental wellbeing that relates to practices which nourish your mind, support mental clarity, cultivate positive thinking and mental robustness, while managing negative thoughts, stress, anxiety and inner critical thoughts and negative self-talk. Practices for mental self-care involve fostering a relationship with your mind and internal voice, such as managing negative self-talk and practising positive thinking techniques. Further information on these practices can be found in Chapter 8: Self-Sabotage and Inner Critic.

Social self-care supports the dimension of social wellbeing that relates to practices which nurture and maintain healthy relationships that are supportive, respectful and enriching to your life. Practices for social wellbeing involve fostering healthy relationships with others, which can be nurtured through healthy boundaries, fulfilling your responsibilities and duties towards others, and building safe and emotionally intimate, robust and available relationships. Further information on these practices can be found in Section Three: Relationship with Others.

Physical self-care supports the dimension of physical wellbeing that relates to practices which support and take care of your physical body and health, as an obligation and trust (Amanah) from Allah (swt). Practices for physical wellbeing involve fostering a positive, loving and caring relationship with your body, which can be nurtured through practices such as good hygiene and cleanliness routines, balanced diet and exercise activities, and good sleep habits. Examples are shared in Chapter 4: Self-Care Planning for Wellbeing.

Professional and financial self-care supports the dimension of professional and financial wellbeing that relates to practices which support a working lifestyle that considers your self-care needs both at work and away from work in your personal life. Practices for professional and financial wellbeing involve fostering a healthy balance between your work and personal life, and healthy relationships at work, which can be nurtured through practices such as clear communication, working in roles and professions ethically, earning 'halal' income, taking regular breaks, healthy work and professional boundaries, setting clear boundaries between work and your personal time, and managing your finances and financial goals. Examples are shared in Chapter 4: Self-Care Planning for Wellbeing.

A self-care practice for wellbeing is about balance, finding a middle path and avoiding extremes. A self-care approach to wellbeing is holistic, taking into consideration all the dimensions of wellbeing and attending to all of them equally. By fulfilling your self-care and wellbeing needs, you can look after yourself and your relationships, fulfilling your responsibilities, duties and obligations to yourself and others.

By creating a self-care plan, you can establish a long-term and sustainable wellbeing plan for your own growth. Through setting intentions and being consciously intentional in your self-care and wellbeing plans, actions and relationships, you can support yourself to live with purpose, to lead a successful life in this life and in the Hereafter (Akihrah). In the next chapter you can start your self-care planning with intention to fulfil your wellbeing needs. Throughout this book, you will discover many practices to support your self-care for balanced, healthy wellbeing.

REFLECTIONS

What are your reflections from this chapter?

. . . .

. . . .

. . . .

What is your current practice or relationship with your self-care?

. . . .

. . . .

. . . .

What might you now consider in your self-care? What would you do? How might you do that?

. . . .

. . . .

. . . .

What would you like to add to your self-care practice? You can add this to your self-care plan (in Chapter 4 and available to download).

. . . .

. . . .

. . . .

Self-Care Planning for Wellbeing

Creating a self-care plan

Being intentional and creating a self-care plan for your wellbeing is essential in identifying how to meet your self-care and wellbeing needs, and how to build a sustainable and consistent habit of meeting these needs.

The following self-care plan for wellbeing template can act as your framework to identify what you can practically do to support your wellbeing. You will notice that there are the six different categories of self-care and each circle within the wheel relates to the three wellbeing relationship dimensions (relationship with Allah (swt), relationship with self and relationship with others). This is because each of the three wellbeing relationship dimensions can be met through the six different self-care categories.

For example, you can nurture your relationship with others through social self-care activities such as meeting up with friends, or a physical self-care activity such as going to the gym, or an emotional self-care activity of putting in healthy boundaries with others. You can choose how each wellbeing relationship is met through which types of self-care activity.

Please note that many self-care activities will overlap across the three relationships and six components of wellbeing and may not neatly fit into one specific relationship or wellbeing component. Don't worry about which specific combination of wellbeing component and relationship a self-care activity fits into. What is important is that you are giving attention to all six components of your wellbeing and nurturing all three relationships, through self-care activities that feel supportive and nurturing to you.

Your unique self-care plan

Your self-care plan for wellbeing will be unique to you. Identify the practices to nurture each relationship and wellbeing component, and fill in each segment of the plan. A self-care plan template is provided for you to fill in, followed by an example self-care plan with ideas and suggestions of self-care practices.

It is essential to remember that self-care is about you meeting your own wellbeing needs, which may not look the same as anyone else's, so some of the examples suggested may not directly or deeply resonate or apply to you, whereas others will. Once you recognize what your self-care needs are and how to practically meet them, you can begin to create a self-care habit and routine for yourself.

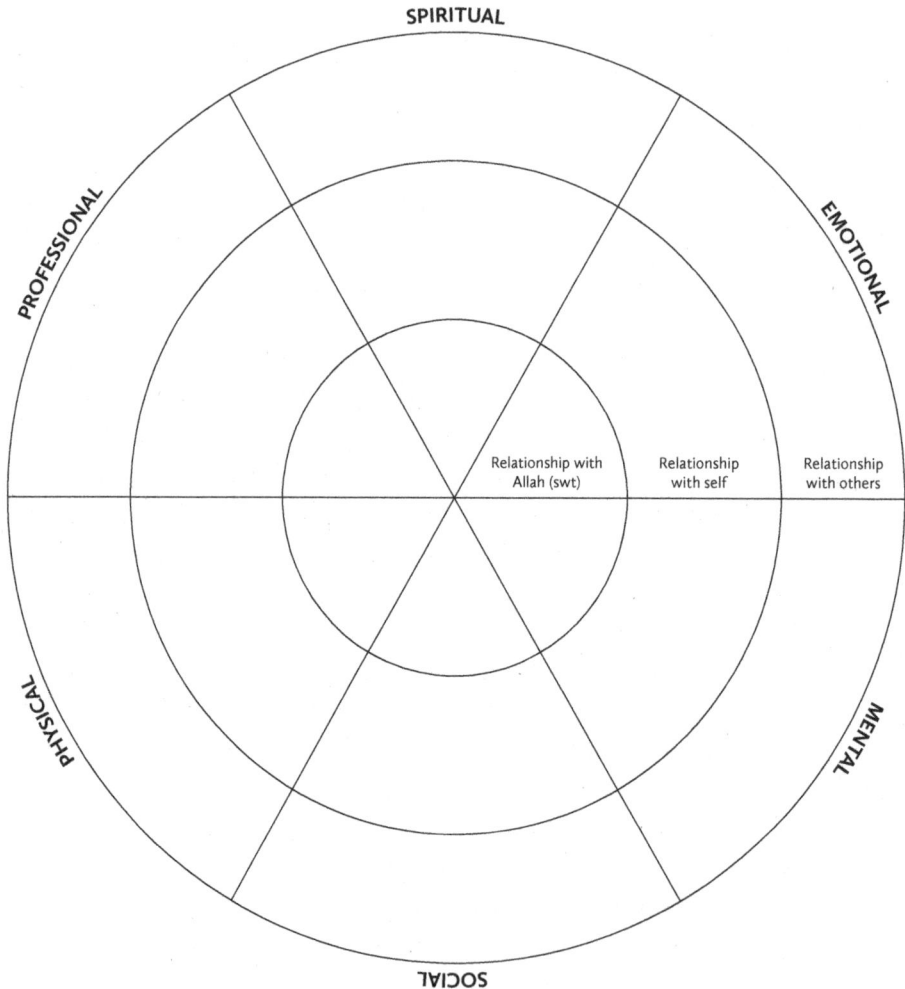

Self-care plan for wellbeing

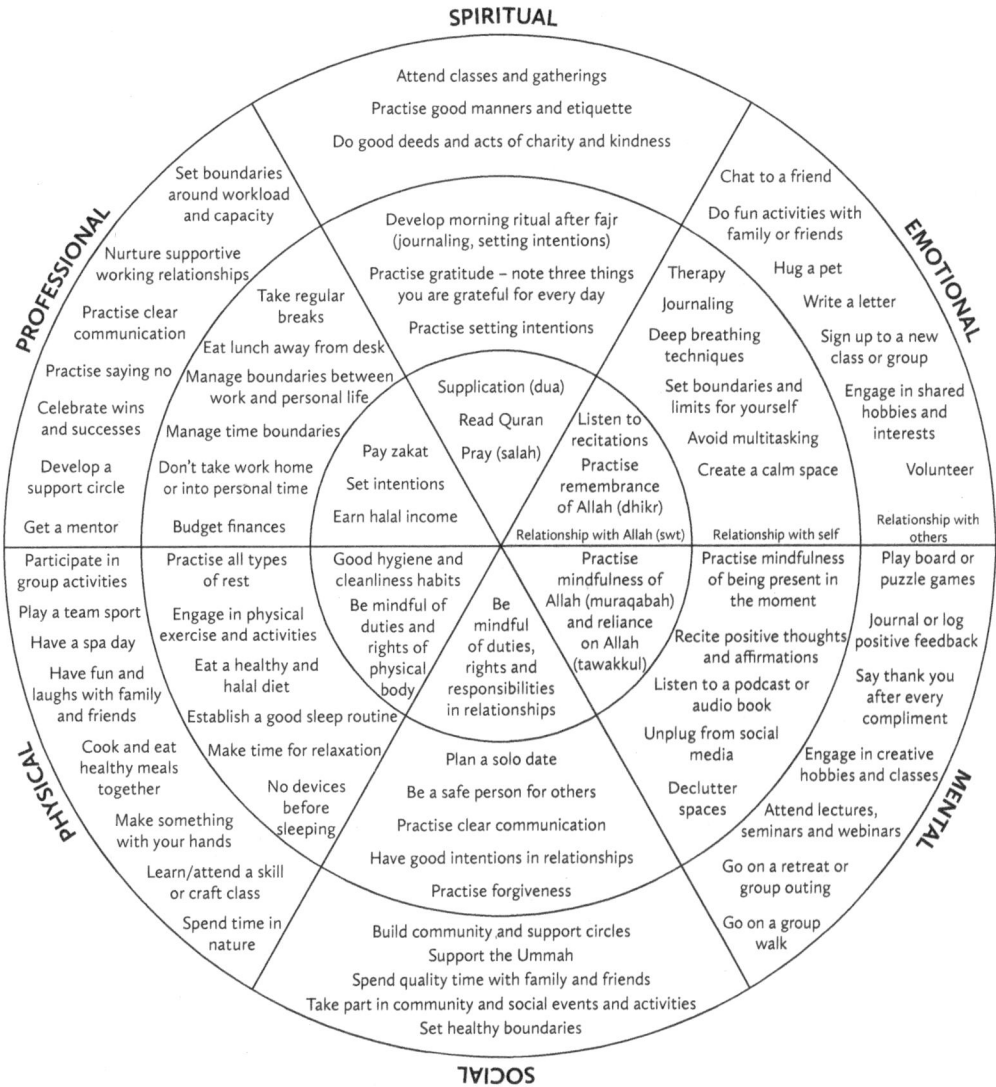

SPIRITUAL

Attend classes and gatherings

Practise good manners and etiquette

Do good deeds and acts of charity and kindness

PROFESSIONAL

Set boundaries around workload and capacity

Nurture supportive working relationships

Practise clear communication

Practise saying no

Celebrate wins and successes

Develop a support circle

Get a mentor

Take regular breaks

Eat lunch away from desk

Manage boundaries between work and personal life

Manage time boundaries

Don't take work home or into personal time

Budget finances

Develop morning ritual after fajr (journaling, setting intentions)

Practise gratitude – note three things you are grateful for every day

Practise setting intentions

Supplication (dua)

Read Quran

Pray (salah)

Pay zakat

Set intentions

Earn halal income

Listen to recitations

Practise remembrance of Allah (dhikr)

Relationship with Allah (swt)

EMOTIONAL

Chat to a friend

Do fun activities with family or friends

Therapy

Journaling

Deep breathing techniques

Hug a pet

Write a letter

Sign up to a new class or group

Set boundaries and limits for yourself

Avoid multitasking

Create a calm space

Engage in shared hobbies and interests

Volunteer

Relationship with self

Relationship with others

Practise mindfulness of Allah (muraqabah) and reliance on Allah (tawakkul)

Practise mindfulness of being present in the moment

Recite positive thoughts and affirmations

Listen to a podcast or audio book

Unplug from social media

Play board or puzzle games

Journal or log positive feedback

Say thank you after every compliment

Engage in creative hobbies and classes

Attend lectures, seminars and webinars

Go on a retreat or group outing

Go on a group walk

MENTAL

PHYSICAL

Participate in group activities

Play a team sport

Have a spa day

Have fun and laughs with family and friends

Cook and eat healthy meals together

Make something with your hands

Learn/attend a skill or craft class

Spend time in nature

Practise all types of rest

Engage in physical exercise and activities

Eat a healthy and halal diet

Establish a good sleep routine

Make time for relaxation

No devices before sleeping

Good hygiene and cleanliness habits

Be mindful of duties and rights of physical body

Be mindful of duties, rights and responsibilities in relationships

Plan a solo date

Be a safe person for others

Practise clear communication

Have good intentions in relationships

Practise forgiveness

Declutter spaces

Build community and support circles

Support the Ummah

Spend quality time with family and friends

Take part in community and social events and activities

Set healthy boundaries

SOCIAL

Self-care plan for wellbeing (with examples)

Weekly self-care routine

A weekly self-care routine may be helpful to create and establish your self-care practices into a regular self-care habit and routine. The template is also available to download and re-use as needed.

Throughout the following chapters, you will find ways to support your wellbeing and relationship dimensions. As you discover new self-care practices, come back and keep adding those self-care activities to your self-care plan and weekly self-care routine.

WEEKLY SELF-CARE ROUTINE

Day	Self-care activity	Time	Notes/reflections
Monday			
Tuesday			
Wednesday			
Thursday			
Friday			
Saturday			
Sunday			

REFLECTIONS

What are your reflections from this chapter?

. . . .

. . . .

. . . .

What self-care practices would you like to start? What would you do? How might you do that?

. . . .

. . . .

. . . .

Are there any self-care practices that you are already doing but could be more intentional about? What would you do? How might you do that?

. . . .

. . . .

. . . .

What actions or practices can you add to your self-care plan (see above)?

. . . .

. . . .

. . . .

How can you further support your three relationship dimensions?

1. Relationship with Allah (swt):

. . . .

. . . .

2. Relationship with self:

. . . .

. . . .

3. Relationship with others:

. . . .

. . . .

Relationship with Allah (swt)

'And when My slaves ask you (O Muhammad SAW) concerning Me, then (answer them), I am indeed near (to them by My Knowledge). I respond to the invocations of the supplicant when he calls on Me (without any mediator or intercessor). So let them obey Me and believe in Me, so that they may be led aright.' (2:186)

CHAPTER 5

Relationship with Allah (swt)

Cultivating your relationship and connection to Allah (swt) is a deeply pro-found and fulfilling journey that nurtures your wellbeing. Nurturing a deep and fulfilling connection with the Creator brings purpose, inner peace and moral clarity to your life. It involves belief, trust and reliance on His divine guidance, alongside practices that strengthen this relationship.

Your relationship with Allah (swt) is central to your wellbeing, as it aligns your thoughts, emotions and actions with the principles of Islam and supports you to establish and maintain a deep connection with Allah (swt), which man-ifests in every aspect of your daily life and identity.

Through different spiritual practices, and wellbeing and self-care activities, you can support and nurture this connection for your optimal wellbeing.

Principles and practices to cultivate your relationship with Allah (swt)

Principles and practices to cultivate your relationship with Allah (swt) for spiritual health and holistic wellbeing include:

- **The Oneness of Allah (swt) (Tawhid):** Understanding that everything in existence belongs solely to Allah (swt), the Creator, supports the sense of you belonging to Allah (swt) and that your life is entrusted to you by Allah (swt). It means living in accordance with His guidance and being accountable for every action, and fosters a sense of trust, gratitude and reliance on Him.

  > Say (O Muhammad (Peace be upon him)): He is Allah, (the) One.
  >   Allah-us-Samad (The Self-Sufficient Master, Whom all creatures need, He neither eats nor drinks).
  >   He begets not, nor was He begotten.
  >   And there is none co-equal or comparable unto Him. (112:1–4)

- **Consciousness of Allah (swt) (Taqwa):** Being consciously aware of Allah (swt) in your daily life supports you to always check your intentions and to align your thoughts, actions and decisions to your faith, duties and purpose, which works as a moral compass and anchor, providing direction and purpose to Allah's (swt) guidance. This fosters clarity, peace and certainty in your life.

  > Say (O Muhammad SAW): 'O My slaves who believe (in the Oneness of Allah Islamic Monotheism), be afraid of your Lord (Allah) and keep your duty to Him. Good is (the reward) for those who do good in this world, and Allah's earth is spacious (so if you cannot worship Allah at a place, then go to another)! Only those who are patient shall receive their rewards in full, without reckoning.' (39:10)

- **Awareness of purpose:** A meaningful relationship with Allah (swt) starts by recognizing that life has a divine purpose. Allah (swt) created humans to serve and worship Him, fulfil His commands and strive to live a life of virtue in preparation for the Hereafter (Akhirah). Recognizing that you have purpose and direction in this life, as you look towards the next life (Hereafter), this understanding provides you with clarity and direction in life, as well as helping you prioritize what really matters.

  > As for those who strive hard in Us (Our Cause), We will surely guide them to Our Paths (i.e. Allah's Religion – Islamic Monotheism). And verily, Allah is with the Muhsinun (good-doers). (29:69)

- **Submission to Allah's Will:** Accepting and submitting to Allah's (swt) wisdom and plan instils a sense of trust in Him, which decreases feelings of anxiety and uncertainty about the future.

  > Say: 'Nothing shall ever happen to us except what Allah has ordained for us. He is our Maula (Lord, Helper and Protector).' And in Allah let the believers put their trust. (9:51)

- **Worship:** Building and strengthening your relationship with Allah (swt) deepens your heart's connection and direct communication to Him, keeping you guided and inspired in your daily purpose. Through practices such as reading the Quran, listening to recitations and learning the 99 names of Allah (swt), and fasting, you nurture your connection to Him.

You (Alone) we worship, and you (Alone) we ask for help (for each and everything). (1:5)

- **Prayer (Salah):** As the foundation of your spiritual self-care, prayer offers a structure to your daily routine through the five prayer times and consistently supports your connection to Allah (swt), which fosters a practice of mindfulness and peace.

   And seek help in patience and As-Salat (the prayer) and truly it is extremely heavy and hard except for Al-Khashi'un [i.e. the true believers in Allah – those who obey Allah with full submission, fear much from His Punishment, and believe in His Promise (Paradise, etc.) and in His Warnings (Hell, etc.)]. (2:45)

- **Remembrance of Allah (swt) (Dhikr):** Remembering and praising Allah (swt) through words such as 'SubhanAllah (swt)' (Glory be to Allah (swt)) and 'Alhamdulillah' (Praise be to Allah (swt)) fosters tranquillity.

   O you who believe! Remember Allah with much remembrance. And glorify His Praises morning and afternoon [the early morning (Fajr) and 'Asr prayers]. (33:41–42)

- **Supplication (Dua):** Calling upon Allah (swt) or asking for help, guidance or blessings from him supports a cathartic practice and emotional release of reaching out and leaving your 'asks' with Allah (swt), which brings about hope and peace of mind, and reduces stress and anxiety, which fosters a reliance on Allah (swt).

   Invoke your Lord with humility and in secret. He likes not the aggressors. And do not do mischief on the earth, after it has been set in order, and invoke Him with fear and hope; Surely, Allah's Mercy is (ever) near unto the good-doers. (7:55–56)

- **Mindfulness of Allah (swt) (Muraqabah):** Acknowledging and being mindful of Allah's (swt) constant presence, who watches and is all-knowing of your thoughts, intentions, actions and behaviours, supports acknowledgement of how you are showing up in your everyday life, and helps you to be accountable and responsible for yourself, to stay present in the moment and not to over-worry or become anxious of the future.

It nurtures you to be more self-reflective and self-aware, and to deepen your connection to Allah (swt) in the here and now.

> O you who believe! Fear Allah and keep your duty to Him. And let every person look to what he has sent forth for the morrow, and fear Allah. Verily, Allah is All-Aware of what you do. (59:18)

- **Reliance on Allah (swt) (Tawakkul):** This means placing complete and full trust and reliance in Allah (swt), while intentionally and proactively fulfilling your duties and responsibilities. This is the spiritual reliance you have on Allah (swt) to support you to navigate your daily life with confidence and knowledge that His wisdom and power is present in every moment, knowing no one has more power than Him, and that whatever happens in your life, Allah (swt) is there looking out for you and protecting you. Relying on Allah (swt) invites a calmness and inner peace from the belief that you are never alone, and life is unfolding in accordance with Allah's (swt) plan for you. Cultivating trust in Allah (swt) allows you to surrender and let go of control, instead finding comfort in His plan for you.

> But if they turn away, say (O Muhammad SAW): 'Allah is sufficient for me. La ilaha illa Huwa (none has the right to be worshipped but He), in Him I put my trust and He is the Lord of the Mighty Throne.' (9:129)

- **Patience (Sabr):** By practising self-control and perseverance, especially when facing any challenges or difficulties, patience supports you to feel calm and grounded, without despair and helplessness, knowing that you are reliant on Allah (swt) and submitting to and accepting His plan for you. Patience is not passive but asks you to sit with trust in Allah's (swt) plan and belief that everything happens for a reason and at the time it is meant to happen, alongside taking proactive action in activities or tasks that support you to manage or navigate the challenges you face.

> O you who believe! Seek help in patience and As-Salat (the prayer). Truly! Allah is with As-Sabirin (the patient ones, etc.). (2:153)

- **Gratitude (shukr):** Practising gratefulness for Allah's (swt) blessings reduces or removes feelings of greed, entitlement or unhappiness, and instead fosters a positive appreciation for the abundance of Allah's (swt) blessings that you have been blessed with. Gratitude pivots you from a 'lack' mindset, of what you don't have, and moves you to an abundant mindset, which acknowledges the abundance of what you do have. When practising gratitude consistently, you can count your blessings during both good and bad times, recognizing that blessings are always present, no matter what you are experiencing. This encourages a positive and hopeful outlook during both good and hard times. Practise naming three things you are grateful for each day. (See Chapter 6: Gratitude for further support.)

> And (remember) when your Lord proclaimed: 'If you give thanks (by accepting Faith and worshipping none but Allah), 1 will give you more (of My Blessings)...' (14:7)

- **Moral character and conduct (Akhlaq):** By aligning yourself to an ethical framework, you intentionally and consciously show up in your everyday life, and relationship with yourself, with others and with Allah (swt), with good moral conduct and character, such as being kind, humble, patient and compassionate. You can develop a relationship with Allah (swt), which is filled with sincerity and intention to connect and worship. In relationship with yourself and others, you become mindful of how you are showing up and with the intention of being of good character.

> Indeed in the Messenger of Allah (Muhammad SAW) you have a good example to follow for him who hopes in (the Meeting with) Allah and the Last Day and remembers Allah much. (33:21)

- **Intentions (Niyyat):** By consciously setting intentions for your actions and behaviours, you can set a direction of 'travel' for your day and how you would like your day to unfold, what you would like to do and how you would like to show up in your everyday life.

> Allah will not call you to account for that which is unintentional in your oaths, but He will call you to account for that which your hearts have earned. And Allah is Oft-Forgiving, Most-Forbearing. (2:225)

- **Accountability (Hisa):** This means holding responsibility for your actions, intentions and deeds in this life and on the Day of Judgement, and knowing that you will be answerable before Allah (swt). By holding accountability for your own actions, you support your self-awareness and self-reflection to live, be and do, as aligned with and according to faith, which builds integrity in your character and how you choose to be, act and show up in this life.

> So whosoever does good equal to the weight of an atom (or a small ant), shall see it. And whosoever does evil equal to the weight of an atom (or a small ant), shall see it. (99:7–8)

- **Forgiveness and mercy:** Being aware of Allah's (swt) mercy and forgiveness towards your mistakes and sins supports the development of your own self-compassion and moves you away from despair, to seek repentance (Tawbah), and towards His mercy and hope for a fulfilled and blessed life. (See Chapter 14: Self-Compassion for further support.)

> And whoever does evil or wrongs himself but afterwards seeks Allah's Forgiveness, he will find Allah Oft-Forgiving, Most Merciful. (4:110)

- **Muslim community (Ummah):** Building a relationship with your fellow Muslim brothers and sisters provides you with connection, community, mutual support and shared experiences, which support your wellbeing. Creating your own support circle and immediate community supports you to cultivate healthy, safe relationships and connections, which can nurture your wellbeing. Attending groups, classes and gatherings together not only builds your community but also supports your spiritual growth. (See Chapter 24 for further support on creating your support circle.)

> The believers, men and women, are Auliya' (helpers, supporters, friends, protectors) of one another, they enjoin (on the people) Al-Ma'ruf (i.e. Islamic Monotheism and all that Islam orders one to do), and forbid (people) from Al-Munkar (i.e. polytheism and disbelief of all kinds, and all that Islam has forbidden); they perform As-Salat (Iqamat-as-Salat) and give the Zakat, and obey Allah and His Messenger. Allah will have His Mercy on them. Surely Allah is All-Mighty, All-Wise. (9:71)

- **Acts of charity (Sadaqah and zakat):** Supporting others through charitable acts fosters your generosity, empathy, kindness and duty of care towards others. Giving to charity supports you to have greater humility for what you have, cultivates your gratitude and lowers your greed and selfishness, as you nourish your compassion for other people and their struggles. Giving zakat (charity obligation) also strengthens your connection to Allah (swt) in fulfilling your duty and greater sense of purpose.

Those who spend their wealth in the Cause of Allah, and do not follow up their gifts with reminders of their generosity or with injury, their reward is with their Lord. On them shall be no fear, nor shall they grieve. (2:262)

Additional Quran verses for guidance and support

Here is a selection of additional Quran verses for guidance and support of your wellbeing, to recite and remind yourself of during times of need and remembrance.

Trust in Allah (swt) (Tawakkul)

Then when you have taken a decision, put your trust in Allah, certainly, Allah loves those who put their trust (in Him). (3:159)

The believers are only those who, when Allah is mentioned, feel a fear in their hearts and when His Verses (this Quran) are recited unto them, they (i.e. the Verses) increase their Faith; and they put their trust in their Lord (Alone). (8:2)

And put your trust in Allah, and Sufficient is Allah as a Wakil (Trustee, or Disposer of affairs). (33:3)

Compassion and mercy

When those who believe in Our Ayat (proofs, evidences, verses, lessons, signs, revelations, etc.) come to you, say: 'Salamun 'Alaikum' (peace be on you); your Lord has written Mercy for Himself, so that, if any of you does evil in ignorance, and thereafter repents and does righteous good deeds (by obeying Allah), then surely, He is Oft-Forgiving, Most Merciful. (6:54)

My Mercy embraces all things. (7:156)

And if you would count the graces of Allah, never could you be able to count them. Truly! Allah is Oft-Forgiving, Most Merciful. (16:18)

And verily, I am indeed Forgiving to him who repents, believes (in My Oneness, and associates none in worship with Me) and does righteous good deeds, and then remains constant in doing them, (till his death). (20:82)

Despair not of the Mercy of Allah, verily Allah forgives all sins. Truly, He is Oft-Forgiving, Most Merciful. (39:53)

So verily, with the hardship, there is relief. (94:5)

Patience (Sabr)

And certainly, We shall test you with something of fear, hunger, loss of wealth, lives and fruits, but give glad tidings to As-Sabirin (the patient ones, etc.). Who, when afflicted with calamity, say: 'Truly! To Allah we belong and truly, to Him we shall return.' They are those on whom are the Salawat (i.e. blessings, etc.) (i.e. who are blessed and will be forgiven) from their Lord, and (they are those who) receive His Mercy, and it is they who are the guided-ones. (2:155–157)

And verily, whosoever shows patience and forgives that would truly be from the things recommended by Allah. (42:43)

Gratitude

Therefore remember Me (by praying, glorifying, etc.). I will remember you, and be grateful to Me (for My countless Favours on you) and never be ungrateful to Me. (2:152)

O you who believe (in the Oneness of Allah – Islamic Monotheism)! Eat of the lawful things that We have provided you with, and be grateful to Allah, if it is indeed He Whom you worship. (2:172)

Verily! Allah will not change the good condition of a people as long as they do not change their state of goodness themselves (by committing sins and by being ungrateful and disobedient to Allah). (13:11)

And if you would count the graces of Allah, never could you be able to count them. Truly! Allah is Oft-Forgiving, Most Merciful. (16:18)

And indeed We bestowed upon Luqman Al-Hikmah (wisdom and religious understanding, etc.) saying: 'Give thanks to Allah', and whoever gives thanks, he gives thanks for (the good of) his ownself. And whoever is unthankful, then verily, Allah is All-Rich (Free of all wants), Worthy of all praise. (31:12)

Nay! But worship Allah (Alone and none else), and be among the grateful. (39:66)

Mindfulness of Allah (swt) (Muraqabah)

And remember your Lord by your tongue and within yourself, humbly and with fear without loudness in words in the mornings, and in the afternoons and be not of those who are neglectful. (7:205)

Those who believe (in the Oneness of Allah – Islamic Monotheism), and whose hearts find rest in the remembrance of Allah, Verily, in the remembrance of Allah do hearts find rest. (13:28)

And He is with you (by His Knowledge) wheresoever you may be. And Allah is the All-Seer of what you do. (57:4)

Verily! Those who fear their Lord unseen (i.e. they do not see Him, nor His Punishment in the Hereafter, etc.), theirs will be forgiveness and a great reward (i.e. Paradise). And whether you keep your talk secret or disclose it, verily, He is the All-Knower of what is in the breasts (of men). Should not He Who has created know? And He is the Most Kind and Courteous (to His slaves) All-Aware (of everything). (67:12–14)

When distressed, anxious and in need of guidance

And spend in the Cause of Allah (i.e. Jihad of all kinds, etc.) and do not throw yourselves into destruction (by not spending your wealth in the Cause of Allah), and do good. Truly, Allah loves Al-Muhsinun (the good-doers). (2:195)

And of them there are some who say: 'Our Lord! Give us in this world that which is good and in the Hereafter that which is good, and save us from the torment of the Fire!' (2:201)

Allah burdens not a person beyond his scope. He gets reward for that (good) which he has earned, and he is punished for that (evil) which he has earned. 'Our Lord! Punish us not if we forget or fall into error, our Lord! Lay not on us a burden like that which You did lay on those before us; our Lord! Put not on us a burden greater than we have strength to bear. Pardon us and grant us Forgiveness. Have mercy on us. You are our Maula (Patron, Supporter and Protector, etc.) and give us victory over the disbelieving people.' (2:286)

My Lord! Truly, I am in need of whatever good that You bestow on me! (28:24)

No calamity befalls on the earth or in yourselves but is inscribed in the Book of Decrees (Al-Lauh Al-Mahfuz), before We bring it into existence. Verily, that is easy for Allah. In order that you may not be sad over matters that you fail to get, nor rejoice because of that which has been given to you. And Allah likes not prideful boasters. (57:22–23)

REFLECTIONS

What are your reflections from this chapter?

. . . .

. . . .

. . . .

What spiritual principles do you want to be more intentional about? What would you do? How might you do that?

. . . .

. . . .

. . . .

What self-care practices do you want to start doing or developing?

. . . .

. . . .

. . . .

Are there any self-care practices that you are already doing but could be more intentional about? What would you do? How might you do that?

. . . .

. . . .

. . . .

What actions or practices can you add to your self-care plan (see Chapter 4)?

. . . .

. . . .

. . . .

How can you further support your three relationship dimensions?

1. Relationship with Allah (swt):

. . . .

. . . .

2. Relationship with self:

. . . .

. . . .

3. Relationship with others:

. . . .

. . . .

Practising wellbeing that centres your spiritual wellbeing and relationship with Allah (swt) not only strengthens your connection with Him but also nurtures healthier relationships, actions and behaviours with yourself and others for holistic and optimal wellbeing. All wellbeing practices become viewed through a lens and context of spiritual care, which reflects your faith beliefs and values.

CHAPTER 6

Gratitude

What is gratitude?

Gratitude is an essential and intentional practice of your acknowledgement, appreciation and thankfulness to Allah (swt) and for the blessings bestowed upon you by Him. It is expressed through words and actions, in which you recognize Allah (swt) as the source of all goodness. Gratitude is both a feeling, an emotional state of thankfulness and an expression of appreciation, communicating your thankfulness to Him.

It is a form of worship to Allah (swt), to be thankful to Him and for His abundant blessings and to acknowledge His favours and generosity upon you. Recognizing the physical, emotional and spiritual blessings in your life, you develop a deeper connection with Him.

Cultivating and practising gratitude promotes an internal peace and contentment, through focusing on His blessings in your life, your thankfulness for your experiences and your acceptance and submission to Allah's (swt) will and plan for you. This includes gratitude not just for times of ease but also during times of challenge, illness and hardship, as a sign of your trust in Allah (swt) and His wisdom.

Gratitude is not conditional. Conditional gratitude would mean being grateful only when positive things happen to you, essentially being conditionally loving towards Allah (swt) when you think He gives you something 'good'. We need to be grateful for everything that happens – both ease and hardship – when things work out for you and when they don't. To have trust and gratitude in Allah (swt) is to believe that whatever is happening, it is working out for you. When something good happens, when something bad happens, be thankful. There are blessings both in what you have and what you've been spared from or don't have.

There are various ways in which gratitude supports your wellbeing. These include enhanced life satisfaction, mood, mental health, robustness, physical health and relationships. This is because the practice of gratitude intentionally focuses on the positive feelings, behaviours, actions and experiences in your life. Gratitude is a growth mindset, reinforcing you to focus on the abundance in your life rather than looking at what is lacking, not enough or what you don't have. It really is a case of count your blessings.

How to cultivate a practice of gratitude

Here are some practical ways to cultivate a practice of gratitude, to reinforce feelings of thankfulness and an abundant mindset in your daily life:

1. Notice glimmers

Notice those small moments of joy, peace and appreciation.

Glimmers are a reminder of the hope, beauty and abundance in life. It may be a smile from someone, a beautiful flower or a delicious meal. They are the subtle moments of connection to the world and people around you, ultimately reminding you of your connection to Allah (swt) and the beauty in His creations. Practise being intentional to pause, notice and be grateful for the glimmers in your everyday life.

2. Gratitude journal

Keep a daily gratitude journal.

In the morning: List three things you are grateful for that morning to set up a positive outlook for the day. Write down a positive affirmation about yourself, or how you would like to positively think about yourself. Perhaps there is a particular feeling or strength you want to tune into and affirm within yourself, dependent on what is happening for you that day.

At the end of the day: Write down three things you are grateful for that day. This could be a feeling, experience, outcome or person – anything that brought you comfort, happiness, joy or thankfulness that day. Reflect on what blessings you've received and experienced.

End-of-week review: Look back over your daily entries to remind you of the abundant blessings you've received. Express gratitude for them. Use the following daily gratitude journal template to get you started with cultivating a daily gratitude journaling habit.

DAILY GRATITUDE JOURNAL

Morning

3 things I'm grateful for:

1. . . . .

2. . . . .

3. . . . .

Positive affirmation: . . . .

End of day

3 things I'm grateful for:

1. . . . .

2. . . . .

3. . . . .

What made me smile today?

. . . .

. . . .

Is there someone I want to express my gratitude to, and how? (*e.g. gratitude letter/ message or verbally*)

. . . .

. . . .

. . . .

What can I add to my gratitude jar?

. . . .

. . . .

. . . .

What gratitude practice would I like to do tomorrow? (*e.g. gratitude walk, mindful moment or visualization*)

. . . .

. . . .

. . . .

3. Gratitude jar

Decorate an empty jar or box. Every time you feel grateful for something or someone, write it on a piece of paper and place it in the jar. A gratitude jar is a visible and practical reminder of the abundance in your life to be thankful for. Read through the pieces of paper at the end of each month, at the end of the year or when going through a challenging time, to reaffirm your abundant blessings and express your feelings of gratitude.

4. Mindful gratitude moments

Incorporate mindful gratitude moments into your day.

Take a moment to feel and be grateful. Notice what is around you in that moment, which you can be thankful for. Feel your gratitude in your heart.

Use a gratitude prompt, such as a small object, shell or rock, to remind you to take a mindful gratitude moment. You could carry this gratitude object around with you or have it located on your desk or where it would be easily visible throughout your day to remind you to take a mindful gratitude moment.

5. Gratitude visualizations

Visualize what you are grateful for.

Picture what and who you are grateful for. Imagine the positive experiences and people in your life (past or present). Sit with feelings of gratitude and appreciation for them.

Create a gratitude vision board: Create a vision board as a collage of pictures, photos and quotes, to represent what and who you are grateful for. Spend time reflecting on the vision board, to connect to feeling grateful. Have the vision board displayed either where you can see it every day, or in your journal, or somewhere safe for privacy, where you can access it every day as a prompt.

6. Mindful gratitude walks

Take a mindful walk and notice what is around you to feel and be grateful for.

You could incorporate this practice into an already established walking habit or form a new walking habit. It could be a local walk or when travelling in a new city or area. Be intentional and conscious of what you notice on your walks. The nature, wildlife, buildings and sounds. Engage all your senses. Notice what brings you joy or pleasure and what you are appreciating being outdoors.

7. Gratitude letters

Write a letter of thanks and appreciation to yourself or those you are grateful for.

Think of someone who is a positive influence in your life. Write out a letter of appreciation and gratitude to them, expressing what they mean to you and what you appreciate about them. Think of specific examples where they have helped, supported or inspired you. Send the letter to them if it feels comfortable to do so, or keep the letter for your own appreciation and gratitude reflections.

Write a letter of gratitude to yourself, to appreciate your own journey. Be thankful for the abundance in yourself. In your letter:

- Note what you are thankful for in yourself, such as decisions you've made, your strengths and for them showing up when you needed them, or the hard work and effort you have put into your life, studies, work or relationships.

- Highlight your achievements and goals, the challenges you've overcome and positive changes you've made.

- Acknowledge hardships and the strength you've been blessed with to overcome them, and be thankful for the outcomes.

- Celebrate your positive qualities and characteristics, and how they have supported and helped you to be who you are in life.

- Offer yourself encouragement and support for your present and future life. Show yourself compassion and kindness for how you are dealing with things now.

- Offer positive affirmations of who you are and how much you love yourself. Think what your future self would like to say to you.

Reflect on and read the letter in times when you need encouragement or a boost of thankfulness to what you have been blessed with within yourself.

8. Verbal gratitude

Tell someone you are grateful for them.

Instead of a written letter/text, verbalize your appreciation to someone. Practise sharing your gratitude and appreciation when someone shows you any help or support. A simple 'I appreciate you' goes a long way to cultivating compassionate and caring relationships with others. Develop a habit of thanking people more regularly in your life.

Cultivate a gratitude practice and habit that resonates with you and incorporate this in a way that feels natural and fulfilling for you, your relationships and your wellbeing.

REFLECTIONS

What are your reflections from this chapter?

. . . .

. . . .

. . . .

What gratitude principles do you want to be more intentional about? What would you do? How might you do that?

. . . .

. . . .

. . . .

Which gratitude practices do you want to start doing or developing?

. . . .

. . . .

. . . .

Are there any gratitude practices that you are already doing but could be more intentional about? What would you do? How might you do that?

. . . .

. . . .

. . . .

What actions or practices can you add to your self-care plan (see Chapter 4)?

. . . .

. . . .

. . . .

How can your gratitude practice further support your three relationship dimensions?

1. Relationship with Allah (swt):

. . . .

. . . .

2. Relationship with self:

. . . .

. . . .

3. Relationship with others:

. . . .

. . . .

Relationship with Self

'And that man can have nothing but what he does (good or bad). And that his deeds will be seen, Then he will be recompensed with a full and the best recompense. And that to your Lord (Allah) is the End (Return of everything).' (53:39–42)

CHAPTER 7

Building Relationship with Self

What is a relationship with self?

Building a relationship with yourself is the way to attune and connect to your feelings, thoughts, actions and sense of self. By building a strong and healthy self-relationship, you are nurturing your self-esteem, self-compassion and self-value, which support your wellbeing. As with any other relationship, you need to intentionally build and nurture a good self-relationship. It is an ongoing process, as your self-relationship unfolds and evolves over time. But by intentionally investing in this relationship (alongside your relationship with Allah (swt) and with others), you are looking after your wellbeing.

There are many ways to build a good self-relationship. However, you need to recognize that building your self-relationship includes not only giving yourself positive, loving traits but also dealing with your challenging, negative and unhealthy traits too. The chapters in this section will explore some of these healthy and unhealthy traits in further detail, so that you can work towards a strong and healthy self-relationship.

A loving self-relationship is formed from several healthy traits.

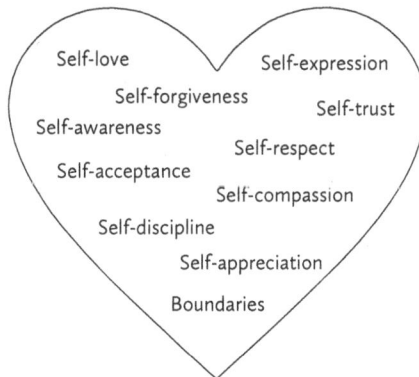

Self-love
Self-expression
Self-forgiveness
Self-trust
Self-awareness
Self-respect
Self-acceptance
Self-compassion
Self-discipline
Self-appreciation
Boundaries

Healthy traits of self-relationship

Healthy traits of a loving self-relationship
1. Self-love
Unconditionally love and celebrate yourself. Self-love is not earnt, and you deserve your own love regardless of what you think you need to do, have done or have achieved to feel loved. Self-love is nurturing yourself fully, without guilt or conditions, showing up fully and authentically in your life for yourself. It is being your own biggest cheerleader. Self-love affirms your worth and value as a person. (See Chapter 10: Self-Love for more.)

2. Self-expression
Share and express your authentic feelings, thoughts, needs and wants. Be honest with yourself about what these are and be open in sharing them with others, so that you feel seen, heard and understood by others and yourself. Be expressive through creative hobbies and interests such as art, painting, writing, crafts or anything that allows your free-flowing expression and supports you to connect deeply to yourself, your passions and your interests. (See Chapter 10: Self-Love for more.)

3. Self-forgiveness
Unconditionally let go and forgive yourself for your past mistakes, failures, regrets or sins, without holding on to shame or guilt. Recognize that everyone makes mistakes, and no one is perfect. Remind yourself of Allah's (swt) mercy and forgiveness towards your mistakes, to support your own forgiveness and move you away from despair towards a fulfilled and blessed life. Only take forward with you what you may have learnt from these experiences, and lean into your future and growth rather than dwelling on the past, carrying the burden or being weighed down by past mistakes and regrets. Focus on your progress and journey now, and look forward. (See Chapter 10: Self-Love for more.)

4. Self-trust
Trust your own gut and decisions. Follow through on commitments and promises, especially to yourself, and trust that you will say, act and show up in the way you intend to and want to and have said you will. It is about believing in yourself and your own abilities, trusting your authentic self to be present and do what is best for you. It is communicating to yourself that you can be reliable, consistent and present for yourself and your own needs. You hold yourself accountable to your own promises, intentions and goals, and follow through on these. This supports you to build trust in yourself with greater self-confidence, robustness and independence. (See Chapter 11: Self-Trust for more.)

5. Self-awareness

Take the time to know yourself, your thoughts, feelings, intentions, values, dreams, likes and dislikes, strengths and weaknesses. Pay attention to how your feelings impact and influence your actions and behaviours, and be honest with yourself about your experiences. This helps you to practise self-acceptance and make decisions based on yourself and what aligns with your values and beliefs. Practise building your self-awareness, to reach yourself on a deeper level and connect to all parts of you. This helps to attune to yourself and more easily connect to who you are and your sense of self. This helps to reduce self-criticism and inner-critic dialogue, and supports a positive self-narrative, dialogue and inner peace. (See Chapter 12: Self-Values and Chapter 17: Emotions for more.)

6. Self-respect

Respect and value who you are – all parts of you. Honour your values, beliefs and goals. Stay true and prioritize what matters and is important to you, without compromising your integrity, conforming to other people's needs or people-pleasing. Setting healthy boundaries with yourself and in relationship with others communicates your respect to yourself, to your time and energy and to your priorities. You avoid compromising your values and beliefs, as you honour them yourself, instead of pleasing others or conforming to external pressures. Self-respect leads to a greater sense of self-worth and self-value that respects yourself. (See Chapters 12: Self-Values and Chapter 16: Self-Growth for more.)

7. Self-acceptance

Embrace and accept all of yourself, both your strengths and flaws. Accept yourself unconditionally. Accept your imperfection and let go of perfectionism. Embrace your uniqueness and whole self, including all those parts that feel not good enough or 'bad'. Sit with all of you. Love all of you. This is the means of cultivating self-belonging, reducing self-criticism and negative self-talk, and embracing your unique self. Of embracing, accepting and valuing the full, authentic and genuine 'you'. It is to 'feel at home' with yourself. To feel safe and connected with yourself. To feel anchored in your sense of self, identity and lived experience. To look within for acceptance and validation. It means letting go of and not chasing perfectionism or external standards and pressures. To know that no one is perfect, and everyone has flaws and imperfections. Who you are is unique, individual and original. (See Chapter 13: Self-Worth, Self-Esteem and Self-Confidence for more.)

8. Self-compassion

Be unconditionally kind, patient, understanding and loving towards yourself, especially when you are going through a difficult or challenging time or when you think you've made a mistake or messed up somehow. Treat and speak to yourself as you would to a friend, with supportive, kind and loving words. Offer yourself self-acceptance of your experiences and feelings, without judgement or criticism. Don't engage or collude with any negative self-talk or inner critic, but instead offer peaceful, kind and compassionate words to all parts of yourself, including any negative voices. This fosters a robustness in yourself during difficult and challenging times as well as communicating to yourself that you are a safe person to be with, a safe 'home' to come back to within yourself, and that you will offer yourself love and kindness unconditionally, no matter what you are going through. (See Chapter 14: Self-Compassion for more.)

9. Self-discipline

Discover your purpose and direction in life. Set your own realistic habits, goals and dreams, and hold yourself accountable for your own goals, dreams and ambitions. Have freedom in what you want to achieve and work towards reaching that. Do this lovingly, without pushing yourself beyond your capacity or being overly critical or a 'workaholic'. Find balance in pursuing your professional and personal goals. Align your goals and habits with your values and beliefs. Cultivate a sense of accomplishment by celebrating your successes, growth and achievements. Create habits and routines that are achievable, realistic and sustainable for you and within your means, ability and capacity, which honour your strengths, discipline and commitment to your purpose and goals. (See Chapter 16: Self-Growth for more.)

10. Self-appreciation

Practise gratitude to regularly appreciate who you are, what you have and what you have to offer yourself and others. This doesn't mean just appreciating what you have materialistically to offer yourself and others, but what you offer in your relationships, through your faith, character, values, beliefs, strengths, skills, knowledge and abilities. Honour your values, strengths and achievements while supporting your growth, determination and attitude to overcome any challenges, burdens or failures. Recognize and appreciate your self-growth, learning journey and capacity to navigate any setbacks or challenges along your path, and see any difficulties as lessons and opportunities for learning rather than as failures and weaknesses. This supports a grateful and optimistic growth mindset to flourish in your life. (See Chapter 6: Gratitude for more.)

11. Boundaries

Setting healthy boundaries for yourself and in your relationships promotes healthy relationships and supports your needs. It is an act of self-love, care and respect to protect your energy and spend your energy where, when and how you want to use it. Your energy and time are valuable and limited; choose to spend them wisely. Boundaries communicate to yourself and others the love, value, compassion, care and honour you have for yourself and for the responsibilities you hold for yourself and are accountable for. Viewing boundaries as essential parts of your relationships, instead of viewing them as rude or selfish, positions boundaries as a loving, respectful and compassionate act of self-care to your relationship with yourself and an act of collective or community self-care with others in your relationships with them. (See Chapter 22: Boundaries for more.)

Together these traits support a healthy and positive self-relationship. One that supports your wellbeing and builds a fulfilling, purposeful life for yourself, creating a solid foundation for inner peace, balance and contentment.

Throughout this book, these traits will be explored for you to establish and practise them as part of your wellbeing and self-being plan and habits.

It is also important to recognize that alongside healthy traits, there are also unhealthy traits and barriers, which can prevent you forming this loving self-relationship. These will be explored further in Chapter 8: Self-Sabotage and Inner Critic, and Chapter 9: Self-Abandonment.

REFLECTIONS

What are your reflections from this chapter?

. . . .

. . . .

. . . .

What traits in your self-relationship do you want to be more intentional about? What would you do? How might you do that?

. . . .

. . . .

. . . .

Which self-relationship traits do you want to start practising or developing?

. . . .

. . . .

. . . .

Are there any self-relationship traits that you are already practising but could be more intentional about? What would you do? How might you do that?

. . . .

. . . .

. . . .

What actions or practices can you add to your self-care plan (see Chapter 4)?

. . . .

. . . .

. . . .

How can these self-relationship traits further support your three relationship dimensions?

1. Relationship with Allah (swt):

. . . .

. . . .

2. Relationship with self:

. . . .

. . . .

3. Relationship with others:

. . . .

. . . .

CHAPTER 8

Self-Sabotage and Inner Critic

What is self-sabotage?

Self-sabotage is self-destructive thoughts, habits, behaviours and actions that undermine your wellbeing, sense of being good enough and self-worth. It is a barrier to a loving, healthy self-relationship. It stops you from working towards and achieving your goals and dreams, moving you into a negative outlook and sense of self.

This can be driven by fears of failure, feeling shame if you are seen to fail at something or proving your fears and insecurities were right, and believing that you are not good enough or can't achieve or 'do' that thing. It could also be the opposite – a fear of success, and beliefs about succeeding that you don't deserve it or it will bring new, overwhelming or daunting responsibilities, expectations or pressures. You may feel guilty and undeserving of any success or sense of achievement from a place of self-doubt in your abilities.

People who self-sabotage may experience low self-esteem, limiting beliefs of feeling not good enough or thinking that any success was down to luck or 'being in the right place at the right time'. This locates the achievement or success externally outside of them, so that any success is due to external factors and nothing to do with their own abilities, skills or knowledge. It could also show up as an avoidance of discomfort or reluctance to move outside of your comfort zone and be in an unfamiliar position of success, achievement, growth or promotion, which can lead to feelings of anxiety, doubt or worry about change and transitions into the unknown and unfamiliar, keeping you holding back or stuck in what is comfortable, familiar and known, even if it means not growing or progressing.

How self-sabotage shows up

- **Inner critic:** That self-critical, negative and pessimistic internal voice, which robs you of your confidence, self-esteem and motivation. It emphasizes your negative traits and tells you who you are in your identity – a failure, not good enough, just lucky, undeserving – and ultimately sets up a pattern of negative self-talk as your default view of yourself and positions success, accomplishments, growth, progress and achievements outside your reach, with you being incapable of closing the gap and bringing them within reach to you.

- **Perfectionism:** Setting impossible and unachievable perfect standards for yourself to reach, as anything else would feel not good enough or a failure to you. Doing a 'good enough' or 'satisfactory' job doesn't feel enough for you, and you push yourself to or beyond your capacity and limits to strive for perfection. Yet the unrealistic standards you set for yourself lead you to a paralysis in your work, feeling stuck or the incompletion of the task, as you fear it won't be perfect and will be harshly judged or criticized for its 'imperfection', causing feelings of shame or inadequacy.

- **Procrastination:** Avoiding or delaying starting or completing tasks or responsibilities, due to a fear of failure or succeeding, feeling overwhelmed or the need for the completed task to be perfect. Procrastination keeps you in a 'stuck' phase before the work starts or is completed, when it feels hard to get going or feel motivated to progress with your work. This fear or feeling stuck opens you up to being easily distracted by other non-important or mundane tasks or activities.

- **Overcommitting:** Saying yes to more tasks beyond your capacity, which leads to feeling overwhelmed or exhausted and being unable to follow through and complete the tasks.

- **Staying in your comfort zone:** Not taking on any new or additional tasks or challenges that will support your growth and move you out of your comfort zone, for fear of failing at the new or additional task or the discomfort of moving into an unknown and unfamiliar zone.

Reflective exercises to overcome self-sabotage

1. Start a journal

Start keeping a journal of your thoughts, behaviours, patterns or underlying beliefs that stop you from progressing. This will help you to identify any pattern to your self-sabotaging behaviours or habits and support you to understand where they stem from. Use this journal template to unpick and reflect on where these underlying beliefs originate. Do you fear failure or success? What keeps you stuck in your comfort zone? What do you believe will happen to you if you do succeed? What impact will success have on you? What do you think will change for you if you did succeed? Do you fear the loss of anything if you were to be successful?

Journal template

Thoughts	Behaviours	Pattern (thoughts or actions)	Underlying beliefs

2. Switch negative thoughts to positive thoughts

When you spot a negative thought arising, capture it and try to identify a positive alternative to it. For example, a common negative thought is 'I'm not good enough'. Challenge this thought or belief by leaning into your strengths and abilities. Instead, affirm yourself with the positive thought 'I'm trying my best'. The positive thought doesn't have to be the opposite of the negative thought, but instead is a kinder and more compassionate thought about yourself in relation to that specific skill or ability. Keep practising turning a negative thought into a positive or more compassionate thought about yourself. This supports the message you are telling yourself that you are self-accepting, valuing and respecting yourself.

Challenging negative thoughts

Negative thought	Switch to a positive thought

3. Identify a task you are procrastinating on

Break down the task into individual steps. Act on the first step. Continue to the next step, focusing on each step at a time. Recognize that fear or discomfort will keep you stuck in procrastination, if these feelings are not accepted as part of your growth and development. It is natural to feel some fear, discomfort or doubt when taking on a new, overwhelming or daunting task, especially if that task is being marked or judged in any way. Challenge yourself to take small steps towards your goal. Rather than looking at the whole task, just focus on the step ahead of you. When you complete any step (no matter how big or small), acknowledge the achievement of completing it and sink into those positive, encouraging feelings of being capable and good enough.

Breaking a task into steps

Task	
Step 1	
Step 2	
Step 3	
Step 4	
Step 5	

4. Name and speak to your inner critic

Give your inner critic a name based on the type of criticism they give you, as if naming a character based on their characteristic. For example, are they 'the perfectionist' expecting you to be perfect but critical when you fall short? Are they a constant 'judge' of your actions, skills and abilities? Or are they 'the critic' – the resident sceptic and dismissive voice of any hard work or effort you put in that's never good enough. Identify how your inner critic speaks about you and give them a corresponding character name. Naming your inner critic helps you to become emotionally and psychologically distant from your inner critic, so that they are not your dominant sense of self; at the same time, you can accept that the inner-critic voice is a part of you. A part of you which you are now intentionally making into a smaller and inferior voice in you. Every time you hear your inner critic speak, you can call it by its name and speak to it. You could say, for example, 'Judge, I hear you, but I am choosing to move forward with compassion and without judgement' or 'Perfectionist, I hear you, but I am choosing to move forward knowing that it is okay to make mistakes and that I am good enough regardless'. Speak to your inner critic character and tell them how you are choosing to move forward in your life with a more compassionate and caring voice that speaks to yourself and about yourself. Try it out and see what happens to your inner critic character, as your authentic voice becomes louder and stronger.

Perhaps you want to write down your inner critic's character name here.

My inner critic character is called: ....

5. Challenge your inner critic

Question the validity of what your inner critic is saying. Ask it, 'Is there evidence for what you are saying?', 'Is what you are saying true?' or 'By moving forward, what can I learn or how will I grow?' Your inner critic can warp your reality, as it sees only through its distorted lens of negativity and criticism, and doesn't hold support or encouragement for your growth or development. Your inner critic is not your cheerleader, but recognize that it can often perform from, ironically, a place of wanting to keep you safe and protected, especially if you hold underlying beliefs that growth, change and success come with a feeling of fear, anxiety or dread. Your inner critic becomes the mouthpiece to stop you from feeling or experiencing these fears, even though those beliefs may be irrational, no longer true or not based in your present-day reality. It's important to challenge your inner critic when its dialogue is no longer true or valid and only hinders you in your self-growth.

6. Externalize your negative self-talk

Project any inner negative dialogue outside of your body rather than carrying those thoughts in your head. Imagine any self-sabotaging thoughts as thought-clouds that pass over your head. Let them float by and away from you. Instead of attaching thoughts inside your head, as belonging to you or defining who you are or your sense of self, detach yourself from them and see them as momentary present and fleeting thoughts. You could practice writing your thoughts down on paper, to project and externalize these thoughts out of your head and into an external 'container', i.e. piece of paper. You can then tear up the paper and/or throw it away, as if you are throwing away the thought as you are throwing away the paper. You can use this technique for any negative thought, inner critic narrative, anxiety or worry. It supports you to lighten your mind and offload the weight and burden of worry, anxiety and negativity in your mind.

7. Practise positive affirmations

As you externalize negative self-talk, practise using positive self-talk, through speaking and reciting positive affirmations to yourself. For example, 'I am good enough', 'I am making progress', 'Every step is an achievement', 'I am learning', 'Mistakes do not define me'. By speaking, reciting or writing down positive affirmations, you are changing the 'script' in your self-relationship of how you speak to yourself and how you think of yourself. Positive affirmations support a positive self-relationship that fosters hope, support and encouragement for your growth, to step outside of your comfort zone and to reach your potential. They will support you to focus on your positives, strengths and abilities. Start by selecting one positive affirmation from the list below to start practising speaking and reciting this to yourself. Write it on a sticky note and place it where you'll see it every day to remind you to speak this to yourself.

POSITIVE AFFIRMATIONS

- I feel secure knowing that Allah (swt) is always by my side.
- I embrace my imperfections and seek Allah's (swt) mercy and forgiveness.
- I am grateful for the abundance in my life.
- I am deserving of happiness and success.
- I choose to let go of fear and embrace love.
- I strive to lead a life that is pleasing to Allah (swt), aiming for the reward of Jannah.
- I am capable of achieving my goals.
- I trust Allah's (swt) plan for me and have faith in His wisdom.
- I aim to embody the qualities of kindness, patience and integrity.
- I am constantly growing and evolving.
- I believe in myself and my abilities.
- I am at peace with my past and excited for my future.
- I am open to new experiences and opportunities.
- I trust the process of life and remain patient.
- I am in control of my thoughts and emotions.
- I am surrounded by supportive and loving people.
- I nurture a heart that is thankful and faithful to Allah's (swt) promises.
- I trust that every challenge I face will lead to greater ease and understanding.
- I attract positive energy and good things into my life.
- I honour my feelings and trust my intuition.
- I radiate confidence and self-assurance.

- I begin every task with the intention of seeking Allah's guidance and blessing.
- I am worthy of love and respect.
- I am grateful for all the blessings in my life.
- I choose to focus on the positive aspects of my life.
- I recognize the beauty and blessings in my life, both big and small.
- I forgive myself for past mistakes and learn from them.
- I strive to show kindness and compassion to others, as Allah (swt) has shown to me.
- I reaffirm my belief in the Oneness of Allah (swt), the Almighty.
- Every day is a new opportunity for growth and improvement.
- I recognize and appreciate the countless blessings bestowed upon me by Allah (swt).
- I turn to prayer and reflection to seek clarity and guidance in my choices.
- I embrace my uniqueness and celebrate my individuality.
- I am worthy of all the good things life has to offer.
- I accept and trust in Allah's (swt) plan for my life, knowing it is for the best.
- I am committed to lifelong learning and growth in knowledge and wisdom.
- I am a vessel of peace and positivity.
- I choose to be kind to myself and others.
- My potential is limitless, and I embrace the opportunities before me.
- I am guided by faith, hope and love in all that I do.
- I have the strength to turn challenges into opportunities.
- My actions align with my values and purpose.
- I am worthy of forgiveness, from myself and others.
- I release the need for comparison and trust my unique journey.
- I am deeply connected to my inner peace and joy.
- I am proud of how far I have come and excited for where I am going.
- I choose to respond with love in every situation.
- My heart is open to give and receive love freely.
- I trust in divine timing and the process of my life unfolding perfectly.
- I am deserving of rest and restoration.
- My mind is clear, my heart is full, and my soul is at ease.
- I celebrate my achievements, no matter how small.
- I trust in my ability to create the life I want to live.

- I choose to be patient with myself as I grow and learn.
- My faith strengthens me and fills me with courage.
- I honour the journey I am on and trust in its purpose.

Perhaps you would like to write down here the positive affirmation you have selected to speak and recite to yourself.

My positive affirmation: . . . .

. . . .

. . . .

. . . .

8. Progress, not perfection

Strive for progress, instead of perfection. Acknowledge that perfectionism is one of the signs of self-sabotage. Perfectionism is unrealistic, and progress is good enough. An advantage to making mistakes is the lessons you learn from it, so your experience of the journey itself towards your goals is part of the experience and growth process for you. Reframe mistakes or failures as lessons to be learnt.

9. Keep an achievement log

List every achievement you make, no matter how small, and identify how you would like to celebrate that achievement. The celebration doesn't need to be extravagant. For example, it could be taking the time to sit with your feelings of success and accomplishment. Keep a log of your successes, goals reached and wins, to remind yourself of positive, confident and proud moments in your life. Practise saying thank you or an act of gratitude to remind you of Allah's (swt) blessings upon you and His plan for you to want and have this experience. Say thank you for the skills, strengths and abilities that have been bestowed upon you, to achieve any and every goal in your life. Use the following achievement log, or if you are feeling creative, create your own log, to fill in. Keep it some-where that you will regularly see it (pinned on the wall or in your journal) to remind yourself of what you've achieved and the blessings in your life that have made this come true for you.

10. Capture positive feedback

To nurture and foster your own internal positive cheerleader, keep a track of the positive feedback and comments you receive from others. This will help you to create a positive narrative and dialogue for yourself of what positives you have, which you can start to say to yourself. You can start to mirror the positive feedback you receive from others in your own dialogue to yourself. Practise receiving and holding on to positive feedback and comments. Don't immediately try to bat away, minimize or downplay the positive comments you are hearing. Learn to receive and accept positive feedback that you are worthy and valued by others. Practise taking the time to really take in and internalize that positive support. Identify how you feel sitting with a positive narrative about yourself. Try to accept not only the feedback itself but also how positive you feel about yourself in receiving it. Use the positive feedback journal below to capture the positive feedback or comment along with how you feel in receiving it and how you feel about yourself. This will help not only to build an inner positive dialogue but also to boost your self-esteem, self-worth and self-confidence.

Positive feedback journal

Positive feedback/comment	How I feel hearing and receiving this

11. Stop comparing yourself

Remind yourself that what Allah (swt) has planned for you, what has been written for you, will be and is yours. Comparing yourself only means to reject, dismiss or be displeased with His plans for you, as you look at what other people have and compare it to what you do or don't have with dissatisfaction. Practise gratitude for what you have been blessed with as well as what you have been protected from. Although something you don't have may look 'good' on the outside, you don't know what it comes with in terms of pressures, worries, burdens or responsibilities, so by not having that something 'good', you may also be protected from any 'negatives' that come with it. Don't fall into a 'grass is greener' mindset. Be grateful for the 'garden' that you are in and what you have been blessed with in your 'garden'.

By challenging your self-saboteur and inner critic, you can develop a positive internal voice, which supports you to have a healthy, positive self-relationship for your wellbeing, instead of sabotaging yourself. As you unpick and reveal your underlying beliefs and barriers to succeeding and begin to understand how your inner critic shows up, you may wish to explore this further in a professional setting, with a therapist, to support you to reflect and process the root causes of your self-sabotage and inner-critic behaviours and habits, and to develop a positive relationship with succeeding in any area of your life.

REFLECTIONS

What are your reflections from this chapter?

. . . .

. . . .

. . . .

How does your inner critic or self-sabotage show up?

. . . .

. . . .

. . . .

How will you challenge your inner critic or self-saboteur? Which practices do you want to start doing or developing to overcome your inner critic? What would you do? How might you do that?

. . . .

. . . .

. . . .

Are there any practices that you are already doing but could be more intentional about? What would you do? How might you do that?

. . . .

. . . .

. . . .

Are there any self-growth goals you want to set for yourself, to support you in challenging your self-sabotage and inner-critic habits?

. . . .

. . . .

. . . .

What actions or practices can you add to your self-care plan (see Chapter 4)?

. . . .

. . . .

. . . .

How can these practices and exercises further support your three relationship dimensions?

1. Relationship with Allah (swt):

. . . .

. . . .

2. Relationship with self:

. . . .

. . . .

3. Relationship with others:

. . . .

. . . .

CHAPTER 9

Self-Abandonment

What is self-abandonment?

Self-abandonment is when you abandon your own needs, feelings, goals, desires, boundaries or general self-care, alongside beliefs that you don't deserve to put yourself first and prioritize yourself. It is a form of neglect or disconnection from yourself, prioritizing other people and their needs above your own. When you self-abandon, it takes a toll on your wellbeing, leading to feelings of discontent, unfulfilment, resentment or a sense of loss and emptiness.

Self-abandonment can also be seen as self-oppression. An oppression of yourself, minimizing, marginalizing and dismissing your needs, wants and desires or your own life, in favour of centring other people's needs and priorities. It shows up as a submissive relational position of over-apologizing, over-justifying or negating your needs or feelings in relation to other people. It places your needs last and works to make others comfortable and looked after by putting them first. Any time your needs are being met, you may feel guilty or apologetic or feel a need to justify your actions.

It also shows up in relationships as looking to others for approval or validation, struggling to say no, difficulty in clear and direct communication, saying you are okay when you're not, avoiding conflict and keeping the peace, placing others on pedestals and viewing their opinion of you as more valid and accurate than your own, and working hard to avoid any unease or upset in relationships.

Self-abandonment (self-oppression) is also an internal process of oppressing your own inner voice. You abandon listening to your gut or intuition, or live in a default 'autopilot' mode of not attuning to yourself. You may ignore your boundaries, compromise your values or beliefs, not meet the duties, rights and responsibilities you have for yourself, your health and your body, isolate yourself and not ask for help, suppress your creativity, criticize yourself with negative self-talk, dismiss your dreams or goals, dim or hide your authentic self, or struggle to advocate for yourself. Self-abandonment and self-oppression are the very opposite of self-love, self-compassion and self-worth. Abandoning yourself is to neglect yourself and the rights, duties and responsibilities placed upon you.

Faith establishes and teaches that every individual has inherent worth and dignity, so offering yourself self-compassion and honouring the rights and duties to look after yourself reflects your inherent worth and dignity.

Healing from self-abandonment is the practice of reconnecting with yourself and having an internal focus on your needs. This includes reconnecting with your feelings, thoughts, values, beliefs, purpose, ambitions, goals and self-care needs. This means to cultivate an internal sense of self of self-worth, self-love, self-esteem and self-compassion, to support a sense of self that feels whole, balanced and cared for. A sense of self that is internally derived and not externally validated. It means honouring your boundaries, feelings, values and goals by prioritizing and fulfilling your needs.

Exercises to reconnect with yourself

You can support reconnecting with yourself by engaging in the following exercises.

1. Identify self-abandonment habits and patterns

Start to identify any self-abandonment behaviours or habits you find yourself doing. For example, this could be avoiding your self-care needs, over-apologizing or over-justifying your actions to others, struggling to establish or maintain healthy boundaries, not putting in boundaries so you continue to say yes and feel overwhelmed, struggling to say no or feeling fearful to say no as you don't want to upset anyone, tiptoeing around others to protect their feelings, not asking for help, putting others first or people-pleasing, going out of your way to help others, especially when they wouldn't do the same for you, playing the peacemaker in relationships, only looking for external validation and not trusting your own self-values or self-esteem, doubting yourself and your abilities, values and decisions, blaming yourself for any conflict or awkwardness in your relationships or taking responsibility for the relationship and overly-investing and committing to the relationship compared to the other person.

To support you to identify your self-abandonment behaviours or habits, use the following self-abandonment habit tracker to identify where, how and why you are self-abandoning. Keep a track of what you are dismissing in yourself or what you doing for others instead of for yourself (see above for examples), when you engage in this behaviour (at what points in the relationship or when you are feeling a certain way), in which relationships you are doing this behaviour, how you feel when you self-abandon and do this behaviour, and any underlying fears or beliefs you have when you self-abandon and engage in this behaviour.

Over time, you can try to identify any patterns to your behaviour and whether they are related to specific relationships, feelings or beliefs. You may wish to engage in therapy to address what is being identified, to help you to process these habits and underlying beliefs, which are driving your self-relationship behaviours of self-abandonment.

Self-abandonment habit tracker

Self-abandonment action/habit (what are you dismissing)	When did you do this?	Who is the action directed towards? (self, partner, family, friend)	How do you feel when you do this action?	Deeper fear or belief related to this action/habit

2. Journal your thoughts

Write down and reflect on your self-abandonment dynamics and how they show up for you. How are your feelings, thoughts and actions externally focused and how do they show up in your relationships? How do they reflect that you are self-abandoning? For example, are you dismissing yourself? Are you neglecting your needs? Are you ignoring your feelings? Reflect on how your self-abandonment dynamic might show up internally. How does your internal dialogue or inner critic show up as being self-critical? What are you saying to yourself that dismisses your feelings, thoughts, opinions or decisions? Do you push them away? Do you doubt, minimize or not follow through on your own decisions? Do you not share these with others and silence yourself? Do you tell yourself negative things or call yourself negative names, such as 'I'm being silly', 'I'm being stupid', 'I'm an idiot'? How does your own internal voice speak down to you, judge you or criticize you? By journaling your feelings, thoughts and actions, you can start to identify a pattern of how you self-abandon. Try to attune to the underlying beliefs supporting this behaviour and self-relationship. Question where has this internal dialogue and narrative come from.

What happened when you started being self-critical and self-abandoning? Who did you hear saying these things to you and what was happening for you that meant you started saying this to yourself?

3. Reconnect to feelings

Allow yourself to connect to and feel your feelings. Give yourself permission to be with your feelings, rather than abandoning them by avoiding, pushing away or denying them. Start to identify the feelings that arise. Name them for yourself, as acknowledgement of you not abandoning yourself and rewriting the script for yourself, of how you meet and honour your feelings. Often feelings are abandoned because they feel 'too big' or overwhelming, or you find it hard to contain them so that you can feel regulated and emotionally safe and stable. By practising connecting to your feelings and emotionally regulating yourself, you can begin to be more comfortable and safer with yourself and your feelings. Look to Chapter 17: Emotions and Chapter 21: Emotional Regulation for techniques and practices of how to reconnect with your feelings and regulate them.

4. Name and meet your needs

Self-abandonment can mean abandoning not just your feelings but also your needs, whether those are spiritual, emotional, mental or physical needs. An abandonment of your needs becomes a pattern and self-relationship of self-neglect. You can begin to resolve this self-neglect and abandonment by starting to connect with your neglected needs. Journal what you notice about yourself, in your daily life or lifestyle, that you are not paying attention to or are neglecting. Ask yourself what it is that you need but are denying or withholding from yourself. What would meeting these needs look like in action or practically? How might you start to implement these actions for yourself? By naming and meeting your needs, you start to prioritize your needs instead of neglecting them.

5. Develop self-compassion

To reconnect with yourself and stop self-abandoning, there needs to be a conscious pivot from a self-neglect and self-critical mindset to one that is compassionate, caring, kind and loving towards yourself. When you start to practise self-compassion, it changes the narrative you tell yourself and your self-relationship about your self-beliefs and values. You become more respectful towards your self-worth and boost your self-esteem. When you practise self-compassion, you stop neglecting and self-abandoning, as you start to recognize your worth and value, as someone who deserves to be looked after and taken care of, instead of being neglected and abandoned. You become more self-forgiving towards any mistakes, flaws or negative beliefs you have about yourself. By practising self-forgiveness, you can drop the shame, guilt or self-blame you may carry in your sense of self or abilities and let go of any judgements, expectations or pressures you put upon yourself. When your inner critic starts to speak up, you can begin to counteract it by meeting it with a compassionate message and dialogue of self-love and self-worth. Think of what you would say to a friend in the same position and say this to yourself. Speak some positive affirmations to your inner critic, to counter-balance its negative narrative with a supportive and encouraging energy. Look at the positive affirmations list in Chapter 8 to find affirmations which resonate with you and you can repeat to yourself. (See Chapter 14: Self-Compassion for self-compassion guidance and practices to support you in developing and practising this more loving self-relationship.)

6. Honour your boundaries

Failing to establish or maintain boundaries to protect your own needs becomes a form of self-abandonment. Whether this is failing to have time for yourself, for your self-care hobbies or for quality rest and relaxation, struggling to create a healthy work–life balance or having difficulty saying no, whenever your needs are not being met because there are no emotional, mental or physical boundaries to protect your energy, time and space, both your boundaries and your needs are being abandoned. Establishing boundaries affirms your needs and prevents self-abandonment and neglect. Putting in boundaries may be challenging at first because they communicate to you and to others that you will no longer neglect yourself, people-please and put others before you all the time. You establish a new, healthy, equally balanced relationship when you assert healthy boundaries. This means identifying your limits of space, energy and time for yourself and others, and saying no to establish and communicate your limits or when you've reached your capacity. This supports healthy relationships not only with others but also with yourself as you now have the space, time and energy to give to yourself and meet your needs for individual self-care activities and practices. (See Chapter 22: Boundaries to support you in establishing and honouring your boundaries and learning how to communicate your limits and say no.)

7. Identify your values

When you disconnect from your core values, beliefs and desires, you abandon your joy, passion and motivation in life and what brings hope, excitement, happiness and direction to your life. By reconnecting to your core values, beliefs and desires, you can start to identify and reflect on what really matters to you.

You can begin to align your needs, your direction in life and lifestyle to your core values and beliefs, so that your life reflects who you are and what you believe in, in your character, behaviours, thoughts, intentions and relationships. You stop neglecting and compromising on who you are in your full, authentic self. You can live and show up in your life and relationships with authenticity, openness and 'truth' of who you are. When you start to reconnect to who you are in your core values and beliefs, you can make time for the pursuits, goals and activities that align with your authentic self and bring your joy, motivation, hope, excitement and happiness in your life. (See Chapter 12: Self-Values to support you in identifying your core values.)

8. Nurture healthy, balanced relationships

When you abandon yourself, you can find yourself in unbalanced, unhealthy, toxic relationships, where others and their needs are prioritized and put ahead of your own. This can show up as an imbalance of the 'give and take' in relationships, where you find yourself doing more or most of the 'giving' and where the space in the relationship is predominantly taken up by the other person and their experiences, problems or drama. You find yourself going out of your way to help the other person or do more for them than they would for you, trying to please them and not saying no; they expect you to say yes all the time and take you for granted in the relationship and what you can and will offer them to meet their needs. Healthy relationships are equal and reciprocal, where you are both valued and looked after, and where your needs are equally met. Nurturing healthy relationships means you can show up fully and authentically in relationships where you can self-express, ask for help, have your needs met and feel seen, heard and valued. Healthy relationships can support the same dynamic in your self-relationship, to stop neglecting and abandoning yourself, and begin to value and look after yourself and your needs. When you start to foster healthy relationships with yourself and others, you may notice any relationship in which you feel neglected, devalued or disrespected, as this shows up as contrary to the compassionate and healthy relationships you are cultivating. You can begin to choose to step back or away from relationships that you experience as toxic or unhealthy for you, and which would collude with you to continue self-abandoning. (See Chapters 23–27 in Section Three: Relationship with Others to support you to nurture healthy relationships and to identify the healthy 'green' flags and unhealthy 'red' flags to look out for in relationships.)

9. Seek therapeutic support

It can be challenging to work through and process your self-abandonment entirely on your own. Therapy can offer the space to explore your self-abandonment and its emotional wounds, to support you to practise self-compassion and self-acceptance, to establish boundaries and to learn about and understand healthy relationships to develop a more self-loving and self-compassionate relationship. Working through these self-neglectful habits and patterns can be beneficial to finding out the root cause of your self-abandonment relationship and to identify where it has stemmed from, to be able to rebuild a firmly rooted self-loving relationship. (See Chapter 28: Therapy for more information.)

Self-abandonment, as a self-neglect relationship, carries self-care and wellbeing deficits for you. Healing from self-abandonment requires you to not only stop neglecting yourself but also to rebuild a new way of relating to yourself and rediscovering who you are. Offering yourself a connection built on love, compassion and kindness supports you to value, honour and take care of your wellbeing and self-care.

REFLECTIONS

What are your reflections from this chapter?

. . . .

. . . .

. . . .

How does your self-abandonment show up?

. . . .

. . . .

. . . .

How will you challenge your self-abandonment? Which practices do you want to start doing or developing to overcome your self-abandonment habits? What would you do? How might you do that?

. . . .

. . . .

. . . .

Are there any practices that you are already doing but could be more intentional about? What would you do? How might you do that?

. . . .

. . . .

. . . .

Are there any self-growth goals you want to set for yourself, to support you in challenging your self-abandonment habit?

. . . .

. . . .

. . . .

What actions or practices can you add to your self-care plan (see Chapter 4)?

. . . .

. . . .

. . . .

How can these practices and exercises further support your three relationship dimensions?

1. Relationship with Allah (swt):

. . . .

. . . .

2. Relationship with self:

. . . .

. . . .

3. Relationship with others:

. . . .

. . . .

CHAPTER 10

Self-Love

What does self-love mean?

Loving yourself unconditionally is at the heart of nurturing a strong, healthy relationship with yourself. It is the practice of holding yourself in high regard, recognizing the unselfish need for love, care, kindness, happiness and compassion. Self-love, rooted in self-respect, self-worth and self-compassion, holds deeply the recognition of your value as a creation of Allah (swt).

When you love yourself, you feel worthy, valuable, seen, heard and taken care of. You align your intentions, actions and feelings with a balanced, healthy wellbeing, which you prioritize. You unconditionally accept yourself, including your weaknesses and imperfection, without judgement or criticism. You shower yourself with kindness and compassion, especially during difficult or challenging times, forgiving yourself and learning from any mistakes you made. You champion and advocate for yourself, for your successes, achievements and growth.

Habits of people who self-love include:

- practising forgiveness
- processing and reflecting on their emotions
- developing a gratitude practice
- developing self-awareness
- investing in self-growth and development
- developing a healthy sleep routine
- engaging in physical activity
- maintaining a healthy diet and lifestyle
- cultivating healthy relationships and connections
- practising honesty and vulnerability with self and others
- developing a growth mindset
- learning and growing outside of their comfort zone
- engaging in acts of charity and kindness
- being a lifelong learner

- accepting positive feedback and compliments.

When there is a lack of self-love or the presence of self-love deficit, it emerges as:

- neglecting yourself and your self-care
- prioritizing everyone and everything else above yourself
- negative self-talk and a dominant inner-critic dialogue
- strong self-criticism
- feeling undeserving of anything good, positive or successful
- dismissing, negating or minimizing any positive feedback or compliments
- striving for perfectionism
- getting stuck in procrastination for fear of failure or not being perfect
- lacking boundaries and ending up being overwhelmed, stressed and overworked
- not finding the time for your interests, hobbies, passions or ambitions.

How to practise more self-love

- **Practise self-compassion:** Treat yourself with the same kindness and patience you would offer to a friend. Support yourself through gentle encouragement and positive affirmations. (See Chapter 14: Self-Compassion for further support and Chapter 8: Self-Sabotage and Inner Critic for a list of positive affirmations.)

- **Prioritize self-care:** Don't view self-care as selfish, but as an essential part of loving and caring for yourself. Look after yourself as a creation of Allah (swt). Make the time for your self-care and wellbeing, as a priority and as valuing yourself. (See Chapter 4: Self-Care for ideas on creating a self-care practice and plan.)

- **Practise self-acceptance:** Let go of trying to be perfect, which is unrealistic. Accept all of you, including what you see as your flaws, imperfections or weaknesses. Unconditionally accept all of you.

- **Accept the good:** Practise receiving any 'good' unconditionally, without expecting to do anything in return. Sit with accepting and holding any good experience, feeling or compliment. Don't minimize the good as 'nothing big or special'. Take in the good as it is.

- **Embrace your uniqueness:** Accept that all parts of you make up your unique, individual self. Don't try to be anyone else. There is only one you, and you are the only one who can uniquely and wholly be you.

- **Forgive yourself:** Let go of past mistakes or regrets – no one is perfect, and we all make mistakes.

LETTER OF FORGIVENESS

Write a letter of forgiveness to yourself, acknowledging past mistakes and to support yourself to let go of guilt, regret or blame.

Reflect on what you want to forgive yourself for – a particular situation, action or decision? Acknowledge how you are feeling and how this has affected you.

In your letter, acknowledge your feelings about the event and the guilt, blame, regret or sadness you felt then and/or now, and any other feelings that arise. Be honest and account for the event itself, what you were experiencing at the time, what led you to that event and why it happened. Offer compassion, acceptance, understanding and kindness towards yourself. Remind yourself that no one is perfect, and what is important is to seek forgiveness from Allah (swt). Explicitly state your intention to seek forgiveness from Allah (swt) and from within your own heart. Reflect on what lessons you have learnt from this event and experience. Note down what you will carry forward with you and your intentions moving forward. End with a positive affirmation about yourself and your commitment to self-love.

After writing your letter you may wish to make a dua for forgiveness. Keep the letter safe and use it as a reminder to practise self-love, compassion and forgiveness.

- **Advocate for yourself:** Honour and stand up for yourself and for your needs. Advocate for what you need from yourself or from others to fulfil your needs.

- **Invest in yourself:** Pour into yourself. Invest in your growth and well-being. Know that you are good enough to spend time and energy on. This might be a specific new hobby, class or interest, or another more consistent self-care practice. (See Chapter 16 for further support on setting self-growth goals.)

- **Practise gratitude:** Regularly focus on the positives in your life. Engage in a gratitude practice to express thankfulness and appreciation for the abundance and growth in your life, shifting your focus from what is lacking. (See Chapter 6 for support to develop a gratitude practice.)

- **Ask for help:** Look after yourself by asking for help when you need it, rather than thinking you need to do everything for yourself. This could be setting aside time to talk to a friend or accessing professional help via a therapist or coach.

- **Set boundaries:** Establish and maintain boundaries that support your needs and wellbeing. Honour those boundaries, without compromising and neglecting your priorities. (See Chapter 22 to help you set healthy boundaries.)

- **Challenge negative self-talk:** Catch any negative or critical self-talk and replace it with positive, affirming, empowering and compassionate thoughts. Speak to yourself with kindness and love. (See Chapter 8 for how to manage negative self-talk and self-sabotage behaviours.)

- **Celebrate success:** Give yourself credit for all your successes, big and small. Celebrate your efforts and achievements. Keep an achievement log where you keep track of your everyday achievements, so you can see over time where you are growing, meeting goals and progressing in your daily self-loving and wellbeing practice.

Self-love languages

You may be familiar with love languages in relationships. There are five distinct ways in which we give and receive love, with your most favoured love language being how you like to both receive love and show love to others. We don't have to choose one from the list of five love languages, but rather we rate them from our most preferred to least preferred love language. You may even find that you have two or three most preferred love languages.

The five love languages are:

- **Words of affirmation:** Positive, loving, affirming words of supports (e.g. said verbally or written in a message or card).

- **Acts of service:** Acting on or doing something for someone else which is helpful, loving or supportive to the other (e.g. cooking dinner, cleaning the house, doing the shopping).

- **Quality time:** Spending uninterrupted, intentional or focused time together and connecting with one another (e.g. watching a movie, going for a walk or going for a meal together).

- **Physical touch:** Showing love through hugs, kisses, cuddles, massage and other physical affection gestures.

- **Receiving gifts:** Being gifted thoughtful and meaningful gifts, irrespective of cost or financial value.

These five love languages can be adapted into five self-love languages (see below). Your favoured love languages in relationships may most likely be your favoured self-love languages, as how you prefer to feel and receive love from others will be how you prefer to show yourself love.

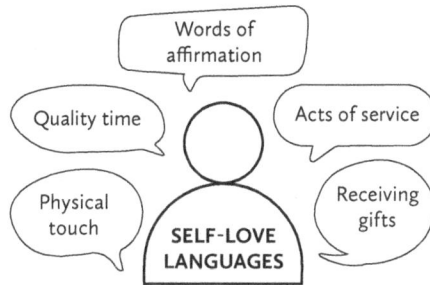

Self-love languages

By recognizing what your preferred self-love languages are, you can implement intentional self-love practices, which will nurture a loving self-relationship to its optimum and support deeper self-connection, awareness and esteem.

How to identify your self-love languages

Think about how you like to show love to others. Do you prefer to spend time with them? Give gifts? Give hugs? Say or send encouraging messages? Or do something helpful for them?

. . . .

. . . .

. . . .

Think about what makes you feel most loved by others. Is it when they give you gifts? Do something for you? Spend time with you? Show you physical affection? Say or send you loving, encouraging and affirming words?

. . . .

. . . .

. . . .

Track your love language communication over the coming weeks. If you are unsure of what your preferred love languages are, keep a log of the love languages you find yourself using and receiving from others. Make a note of which ones feel most loving and caring for you.

. . . .

. . . .

. . . .

Your answers will help you to identify how you like to give and receive love from others and therefore what your preferred self-love languages might be. Remember that you may have more than one primary love language and so have a combination of preferred self-love languages.

My preferred self-love languages are (from most preferred to least preferred):

1. (most preferred): . . . .

2. . . . .

3. . . . .

4. . . . .

5. (least preferred): . . . .

How to practise the five self-love languages

FOR WORDS OF AFFIRMATION

This is the use of positive self-talk and self-encouraging words. Aligned with self-compassion, this is intentionally practising non-judgemental, positive affirmation and self-talk habits.

You can write and create a daily affirmations statement, which you read to yourself every day, or have affirmations visible in your room or office to recite when you see them, such as 'I am worthy of love', 'I believe in myself', 'I am grateful for the blessings in my life'. (See Chapter 8 for a list of affirmations.)

You can encourage positive self-talk, especially when you find yourself starting to be negative or critical. Challenge any negative thoughts that may arise by finding encouraging and supportive thoughts to counteract them – from 'I'm not good enough' to 'I am good enough' or 'I am trying my best'. (See Chapter 8 on how to manage negative self-talk and self-sabotage behaviours.)

Keep a log of wins, achievements and successes to capture and celebrate achievements and successes from the day. Be your own cheerleader! (See Chapter 8 for an achievement log to fill in – also available to download.)

Keep a journal to capture affirming and uplifting words, thoughts and feelings, or positive experiences from your day.

FOR ACTS OF SERVICE

This is you taking care of your needs through practical means, such as practical self-care activities (i.e. going for a walk, to the gym, for a swim, reading a book or having a manicure). It also includes establishing and practising a daily healthy wellbeing routine, such as a healthy, balanced diet, prepping meals, quality sleep, managing and scheduling your time so you are not rushing around, praying on-time and unrushed, and having a balanced work–personal life and time to rest and relax. Make time for self-care rituals, to prioritize and send a message to yourself of your self-love.

Acts of service need not only be physical acts. Setting aside time for spiritual and emotional acts of service, such as practising emotional reflection, practising emotional regulation techniques, practising self-forgiveness or setting goals, is also a self-love act of service for your wellbeing.

FOR QUALITY TIME

This is you prioritizing intentional quality time for yourself, reconnecting with yourself and taking the time to do what you want to do. This can include some regular alone time by yourself for relaxing, reading or engaging in your hobbies or interests, engaging in spiritual or reflective practices such as prayer, journaling or reading, unplugging from social media and phone notifications or setting your phone to silent, engaging in a creative hobby (e.g. drawing, doodling, painting or craft projects), or spending time however you want to without distractions or other responsibilities needing your attention for that time. Developing a habit of setting good boundaries around your quality time will also support you to prioritize this time for you and as a message of self-love to yourself that you are worthy and deserving of this time for yourself. Use the following daily wellbeing journal as a template to support yourself to plan and create an intentional daily wellbeing and self-care routine and habit. The journal template will support you to reflect on your current daily wellbeing habits, set your intentions for the day, assess your day and plan for the next, with you being intentional in your wellbeing practice.

FOR PHYSICAL TOUCH

This is you taking care of and nurturing your body through touch and physical care. This can include exercise, rest and relaxation, quality sleep, self-massage, self-hugging, body-brushing, spa treatments or being pampered, haircuts, grooming and skincare routines, or using sensory toys, fidgets or weighted blankets for relaxation (or stimming).

FOR RECEIVING GIFTS

This is you treating yourself, which can include either physical objects or symbolic gifts that give you feelings of pleasure, love or fulfilment. It could be giving yourself physical gifts which would bring you joy, such as buying a much-wanted treat (e.g. books, clothes, gadgets) or treating yourself to an experience (e.g. going to the cinema, spa, salon, restaurant, on holiday, time off work). Self-gifting doesn't always need to be conditional on achieving a particular goal or milestone, but if your primary self-love language is receiving gifts, then treating yourself to something extra special is a great way to celebrate your achievements and successes. Receiving gifts also includes symbolic gifts such as giving yourself the time to engage in creative projects, hobbies, interests, personal growth and development, and practising self-care habits. It is not just the gift itself that is the expression of self-love but also the time you are taking for the gift itself, which sends the message to you that you are worthy and deserving of your love.

DAILY WELLBEING JOURNAL

Morning reflections

Set intentions for the day

I can make today positive by...

. . . .

How can I feel inspired today?

. . . .

I am looking forward to:

. . . .

Gratitude practice: 3 things I am grateful for:

1. . . . .

2. . . . .

3. . . . .

Positive affirmation:

. . . .

How am I feeling this morning?

. . . .

What self-care activities can I practise today?

. . . .

. . . .

What is one goal or task to focus on today?

. . . .

. . . .

Dua/verse I want to be mindful of and connect with:

. . . .

. . . .

Evening reflections

How have I looked after my wellbeing today?

Spiritual self-care	Emotional self-care	Mental self-care
Social self-care	Physical self-care	Professional self-care

How do I need to support my wellbeing tomorrow?

. . . .

Highlight of my day:
What went well today? What gave me energy?

. . . .

Lowlight of my day:
What challenges did I face? What drained my energy?

. . . .

One thing I learnt about myself: . . . .

3 things I'm grateful for:

1. . . . .

2. . . . .

3. . . . .

Dua or verse I want to be mindful of and connect with:

. . . .

By honouring your preferred self-love languages, you are nurturing your self-love relationship at its optimal best, by communicating and showing yourself love in a way that you can best receive it and take it in.

Based on the above five self-love languages, fill in the self-love language habits template below with ideas for how you can practise your self-love language actions and habits. This is also available to download and use again. Use the self-care examples in Chapter 4 for inspiration.

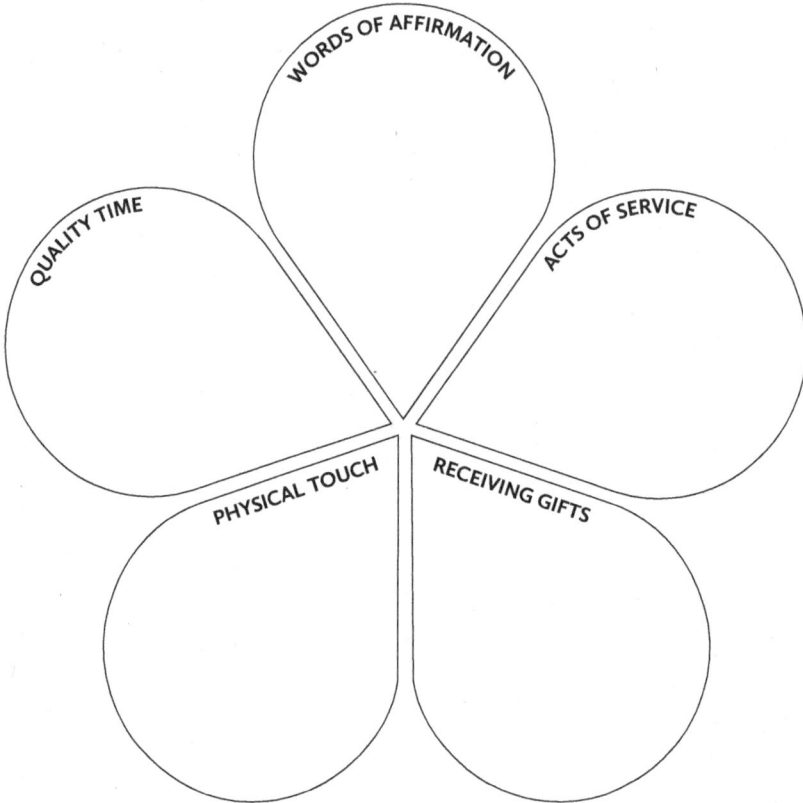

WORDS OF AFFIRMATION

QUALITY TIME

ACTS OF SERVICE

PHYSICAL TOUCH

RECEIVING GIFTS

Self-love language habits template

REFLECTIONS

What are your reflections from this chapter?

. . . .

. . . .

. . . .

How does your self-love language show up?

. . . .
. . . .
. . . .

Which actions or habits do you want to start practising or developing to communicate your self-love? What would you do? How might you do that?

. . . .
. . . .
. . . .

Are there any self-love languages that you are already practising but could be more intentional about? What would you do? How might you do that?

. . . .
. . . .
. . . .

Are there any self-growth goals you want to set for yourself, to support your development of self-love?

. . . .
. . . .
. . . .

What actions or practices can you add to your self-care plan (see Chapter 4)?

. . . .
. . . .
. . . .

How can these practices and exercises further support your three relationship dimensions?

1. Relationship with Allah (swt):

. . . .

. . . .

2. Relationship with self:

. . . .

. . . .

3. Relationship with others:

. . . .

. . . .

CHAPTER 11

Self-Trust

What is self-trust?

Self-trust means to trust your own opinions, beliefs, instinct and decisions. It means following through on your commitments and promises, especially those to yourself, and trusting that you will say, act and show up in the way you intend to and want to. It is having the confidence and belief in yourself and trusting your authentic self to be present, make the best decisions and do what is best for you. Self-trust supports you to uphold healthy boundaries, feel empowered internally to pursue your goals, maintain emotional stability and regulation, and feel emotionally robust to deal with life's challenges.

A lack of self-trust leads to doubting your own abilities and decision making, feeling insecure or vulnerable in your everyday life or future direction of growth and development, and it can lower your confidence, self-esteem and self-worth. This impacts on your sense of self, self-care and wellbeing.

Practices to build your self-trust

1. Take small steps

Set a small goal, step or promise you can make and meet for yourself in the coming days. This will help build your confidence and self-trust when you follow through and do what you said you would do.

Keep a log of your small daily goals or steps in the daily goals tracker below and tick them off as you succeed in meeting each one. As your confidence and trust builds, you can start to set larger goals or steps.

Daily goals tracker

Goal	Target date	Completed	Reflections

2. Pray Istikhara

Before deciding or making a choice, seek Allah's (swt) guidance by praying Istikhara. This prayer is performed to ask for clarity, guidance and blessings in making the right or best choice or decision. Place trust in Allah (swt) that He will guide you in your decision and outcome. A good resource on how to pray Istikhara is available from the Yaqeen Institute website, which you can access at https://yaqeeninstitute.org/read/post/a-guide-to-istikhara-the-prayer-for-guidance or via the QR code.

3. Rely on Allah (swt) (Tawakkul)

After making your decision, place your trust and reliance in Allah (swt), knowing that He controls the outcome and has your best interests in mind, while you continue to complete your obligations or responsibilities for the decision. This spiritual reliance on Allah (swt) supports your confidence to navigate your self-trust and decision making with confidence.

4. Make decisions thoughtfully

Try to avoid overthinking or second-guessing your decision. Use a methodical approach to decision making. For example, give yourself a set amount of time to think about your choices, identify three options or choices and make one final decision. Make your decision intentionally and thoughtfully (after praying Istikhara), trusting that whatever comes afterwards, you can handle it to the best of your ability.

5. Tune in to your intuition (gut instinct)

Listen to how you feel when you have an intuitive sense about a decision or towards someone/something. Trust that your instinct is sending you a message about it. Give yourself permission to listen to your intuition and instinct.

Remind yourself of times when you have listened to your gut, and it was right.

Practise tuning in to your intuition when you need to make a yes/no decision. Get two pieces of paper, one with 'yes' written on it and the other with 'no'. Ask yourself the yes/no question. Listen to which answer you are drawn to. Alternatively, stand on one of the pieces of paper (either yes or no or the answer that feels right for you). Does the answer you are standing on feel right for you or not? How you feel standing on either piece of paper may be how you really feel, and your intuition is speaking to you about what the right decision is.

6. Affirm your strengths

Build self-trust by acknowledging your strengths, abilities, capabilities, skills and traits. Make a list of your strengths, achievements and successes. Celebrate them. Trust in what you have achieved, are achieving and can do.

7. Grow from your past

Reflect on your past experiences. Identify times when you made a decision for yourself. Reflect on the following questions:

- What was the situation and decision?
- How did that decision unfold?
- What worked or didn't work in the decision and why?
- What did you learn from this experience and your decision?
- How can you apply this learning to future decisions, judgements and experiences?

Don't stay stuck or focus on what didn't work, but rather concentrate on what you have learnt from it and can use moving forward.

8. Honour your own commitments

Follow through and fulfil your own commitments and promises. The more often you honour your commitments and promises, the more you will trust your own intentions, show up for yourself and value and prioritize your own needs.

9. Practise self-compassion

Be kind to yourself as you start to build and test out your self-trust, especially if something doesn't go to plan or you weren't able to fulfil one of your own small steps, goals, commitments or promises. Offer yourself the grace that you are a work in progress, and no one is the finished article. (See Chapter 14: Self-Compassion for further support.)

10. Establish healthy boundaries

In committing to your own promises and goals, set limits and boundaries to protect your time, energy and capacity. Putting in boundaries supports your self-trust to prioritize your needs, listen to your intuition and reinforce each experience of trusting that you are doing what is best for you. (See Chapter 22: Boundaries for further support.)

11. Practise self-reliance

Remind yourself of each time you rely on yourself for your own help, support or validation. Recognize and trust in what you can do and that you have resources, skills and knowledge to navigate through challenges, difficulties or decisions, which helps to build your own problem-solving abilities, self-reliance and independence for greater self-trust. (See Chapter 10: Self-Love for further support.)

Building self-trust is an ongoing consistent process and relationship with yourself. It is about you proving and trusting in yourself that you are capable and can look internally for self-assurance, place trust in Allah (swt) and move forward with confidence and trust in your intentions, actions and decisions.

REFLECTIONS

What are your reflections from this chapter?

. . . .

. . . .

. . . .

How does your self-trust show up? How do you show yourself that you trust your decisions, thoughts, skills and capabilities?

. . . .

. . . .

. . . .

Which actions or habits do you want to start practising or developing to communicate your self-trust to yourself? What would you do? How might you do that?

. . . .

. . . .

. . . .

Are there any self-trust habits that you are already practising but could be more intentional about? What would you do? How might you do that?

. . . .

. . . .

. . . .

Are there any self-growth goals you want to set for yourself, to support your development of self-trust?

. . . .

. . . .

. . . .

What self-trust actions or practices can you add to your self-care plan (see Chapter 4)?

. . . .

. . . .

. . . .

How can these practices and exercises further support your three relationship dimensions?

1. Relationship with Allah (swt):

. . . .

. . . .

2. Relationship with self:

. . . .

. . . .

3. Relationship with others:

. . . .

. . . .

CHAPTER 12

Self-Values

What are self-values?

Self-values are the beliefs, principles, traits and characteristics that inform and shape your core self. Your self-values are unique to you, defining what is significant, meaningful and fulfilling to you, and guiding you in how you live your life.

Your self-values influence your intentions, character, attitude, actions, behaviours and decisions. Your self-values support you to find and align your purpose and direction in life to your faith values and beliefs, and what your priorities are. They help to create and nurture a life in which you feel fulfilled and motivated towards self-growth and development, increased self-love, self-worth and self-respect, and showing up authentically in your relationships and all areas of your life as your core, true self.

Core values

Identifying your core values helps you to live a life aligned with your faith beliefs, values, purpose and direction, which supports greater wellbeing. As your core values may evolve or change in priority over time, it is important to assess and evaluate your core values throughout the stages of your life, to know that you are living in alignment with your core values because they influence your decision making, choices, what to focus on in life and what matters to you. Below are practices to help you to identify your core values and how to bring them more intentionally into your life and relationships.

1. Identify your core values

Look through the list of core values. Circle the values that resonate with you, your character and outlook on life. Imagine your 'best' self and how your intentions, characteristics and actions would reflect these values. What core values are driving you and influencing your intentions, attitude, goals, motivations and direction? Perhaps think about those people whom you admire and the values, traits, beliefs and qualities they possess and which you appreciate. This may help you to connect with values you would like to foster within yourself. Which core values support you to cultivate a life that aligns with and reflects your faith and faith beliefs and values. This will help you to reconnect to what matters to you and what you would like to focus on, bring into your life and prioritize for yourself.

Core values list

Integrity	Love	Faith	Family
Accountability	Resilience	Curiosity	Trust
Serenity	Compassion	Happiness	Self-respect
Fairness	Peace	Humility	Justice
Authenticity	Connection	Patience	Kindness
Courage	Gratitude	Faith	Service
Responsibility	Fun	Love	Creativity
Self-love	Honesty	Community	Empowerment
Open-mindedness	Achievement	Balance	Success
Challenge	Humour	Security	Determination
Growth	Loyalty	Generosity	Respect
Purpose	Excitement	Health	Exploration
Empathy	Joy	Knowledge	Positivity
Spirituality	Confidence	Tolerance	Adventure
Excellence	Playfulness	Innovation	Boldness
Freedom	Autonomy	Wisdom	Contribution

2. Prioritize your core values

From the core values you have circled above, select the top ten values that most deeply resonate and align with you. Write these in the list below. This will help you to identify the core values which you hold most deeply for yourself, identity and character.

1. . . . .

2. . . . .

3. . . . .

4. . . . .

5. . . . .

6. . . . .

7. . . . .

8. . . . .

9. . . . .

10. . . . .

3. Meaningful core values

Each of your top ten core values will have some meaning, importance or resonance with you, because you've chosen it either as a current core value that you hold true for yourself or it's a value you wish to emulate and cultivate for yourself. It's important to know how meaningful each core value is to you and why it is important. In the table below, for each of your top ten core values, reflect on and describe what each core value means to you and why it is important in your life. How does each core value fit within your sense of self, identity and how you choose to navigate your world and relationships? What place or position or influence does it have in your identity? What is your relationship to each core value and how might your relationship with each core value have changed over time?

Core values made meaningful

Core values	What does it mean to you? What is your relationship to it?
1.	
2.	
3.	
4.	
5.	
6.	
7.	
8.	
9.	
10.	

4. Application of core values

Knowing your core values is one aspect of self-values; another aspect is knowing how your core values influence and show up in your life. How do they show up? How do they influence you? How do you apply them? What is the impact of them in your everyday life, in your decision making, in finding direction, meaning and purpose in your life, in identifying and achieving your goals, in your relationships? Using the table below, reflect on how your core values inform your life. How does each core value show up in your life? How does it influence, reflect and get applied in your intentions, choices, decisions and life direction?

Core values application

Core values	How does this core value show up in your life? How does it influence, reflect and apply towards your intentions, choices, decisions or life direction?
1.	
2.	
3.	
4.	
5.	
6.	
7.	
8.	
9.	
10.	

5. Core values in your three relationship dimensions

Your core values shape your relationship with Allah (swt), with yourself and with others. Your values are reflected in your personality, character, how you interact with others and how you choose to show up for yourself. For each of the relationship dimensions in your wellbeing, your core values will impact and be reflected in these relationships. Using the following table, reflect on how you believe your core values shape and influence your three relationships. How does each core value shape your relationship with Allah (set), with yourself and with others? Which of your top ten core values are brought to the fore in each of these relationships? Which core values are driving each of these relationships? Which core values are most influential in each of these relationships?

Core values in relationships

Core value	How does this core value shape your relationship with Allah (swt)?	How does this core value shape your relationship with yourself?	How does this core value shape your relationship with others?
1.			
2.			
3.			
4.			
5.			
6.			
7.			
8.			
9.			
10.			

6. Practising your core values

Once you have identified your core values, reflected on their meaning and application, and how they are active and present in your relationships, you can begin to be more intentional in how you want to use your core values more actively in your life and relationships. Using the Core Values in Practice table, reflect on how you can practise and apply your core values more effectively and intentionally in your relationships. How can you embody and apply each core value more intentionally in your relationships? What would that look like? What would you be doing differently, more of or less of, to embody this core value? What can serve as a daily reminder for you to be intentional and mindful of each core value? Can you practise reciting positive affirmations that represent any of these core values? Or have a list of your core values pinned somewhere visible to you as a daily reminder. Before meeting with someone or starting a conversation, can you ask yourself what intentions are you engaging in this conversation with? What core values would you like to embody in this conversation? How would you like to show up and be in this conversation? Practise being conscious of your core values and how you want to be in spaces and relationships. Give yourself the opportunity before entering a space or conversation to take a moment to tune in to yourself and bring your core values to the foreground along with the intention to be, do and act in ways that align with your core values.

Core values in practice

Core value	How can you embody and apply this core value more intentionally in your relationships?
1.	
2.	
3.	
4.	
5.	
6.	
7.	
8.	
9.	
10.	

By identifying and embodying your core values, you can be more intentional in creating an aligned life which reflects your authentic self and is purposeful and meaningful for you. Consider revisiting these self-value practices to assess your core values, as they change and evolve, through your life stages and self-growth.

REFLECTIONS

What are your reflections from this chapter?

. . . .

. . . .

. . . .

Which actions or habits do you want to start practising or develop to identify, be intentional or embody your core values? How do you want to reflect your core values in your intentions, thoughts, words and actions?

. . . .

. . . .

. . . .

Are there any core values that you are already practising but could be more intentional about? What would you do? How might you do that?

. . . .

. . . .

. . . .

Are there any self-growth goals you want to set for yourself, to support your development of self-values?

. . . .

. . . .

. . . .

What core value actions or practices can you add to your self-care plan (see Chapter 4)?

. . . .

. . . .

. . . .

CHAPTER 13

Self-Worth, Self-Esteem and Self-Confidence

Self-worth

Self-worth is your constant core belief of your intrinsic value as a person, as a creation of Allah (swt). It is your internal assessment of yourself, as someone unconditionally deserving of love, respect, kindness, care and consideration. Receiving these is not conditionally dependent on your success, achievements or status; rather, you have an inherent value to be loved and valued.

Your self-worth is shaped by your lived experiences, relationships and core beliefs. To build your self-worth means to cultivate a deep, internal sense of self-value.

How to build your self-worth

- **Recognize your self-worth as Allah's (swt) creation:** Remember your existence as part of Allah's (swt) design. This supports you to place your worth outside of materialistic or worldly success. Remind yourself of this every morning as you say your duas upon waking and every evening going to sleep. This helps to give yourself perspective of your existence in the wider picture.

- **Focus on the Hereafter (Akhirah):** Prioritize and strive for intentions and actions that will support you and bring you closer to the rewards of the Hereafter. Your worth is supported by your core values and beliefs, and is helping your future self.

- **Trust in Allah (swt) and His plan (Tawakkul):** Remember that Allah (swt) is the best of planners, and any difficulties or challenges you experience are opportunities for learning and growth, not reflections of your weaknesses, mistakes and worthiness.

- **Set intentions:** Recognize that setting intentions shifts your self-worth from external validation to your relationship with Allah (swt) and His blessings and acceptance. Practise setting intentions for all your actions, behaviours and character.

- **Determine your core beliefs:** Recognize your core beliefs about yourself. What do you believe about your value and self-worth? How do your core beliefs honour your faith? If you have negative or low self-worth, practise positive affirmations that reflect supportive and high self-worth beliefs, as based in the truth that you are inherently worthy and valuable. See the list of self-reassurance affirmations at the end of the chapter and the list of positive affirmations in Chapter 8 to identify positive affirmations you can use.

- **Embrace your uniqueness and value:** Remind yourself of your unconditional inherent value. You are good enough for being you. Practise positive self-talk as part of your daily self-care routine. Have a mantra about your self-worth that you can repeat and come back to. Change your inner dialogue to reflect the love, kindness and respect you deserve from yourself. Avoid negative self-talk; instead, remind yourself of Allah's (swt) mercy and the goodness and potential He has blessed within you. (See Chapter 8: Self-Sabotage and Inner Critic to challenge any negative self-talk.)

- **Practise self-validation:** Acknowledge, validate and celebrate your life, experiences, relationships and choices. Validate who you are instead of what you do. Journal, log or keep a tracker of your life experiences to validate and celebrate yourself. Celebrate what is an achievement to you, in a way that is meaningful to you.

- **Practise self-compassion:** Look after yourself with compassion. Treat yourself as you would a friend. Unconditionally love, respect and value who you are, irrespective of any mistakes. You are worth your love, respect and kindness always. (See Chapter 14: Self-Compassion for further support.)

- **Practise self-care:** Establish a self-care habit. Value your self-care needs (spiritual, emotional, physical, etc.) and meet these needs as fulfilling the trust Allah (swt) has placed on you, for your mind, body and soul. Engage in activities you enjoy, reinforcing your worth in being happy and fulfilled. You are worthy of your time, attention and effort to be looked after. (See Chapter 3 for self-care planning and examples of practice.)

- **Set boundaries:** Value your time, energy and wellbeing. Offer your time and energy where and when it is valued. Practise saying no when it doesn't reflect your worth. Recognize the value of what you can offer to yourself and others. (See Chapter 22 for further support on setting boundaries.)

- **Stop comparing yourself:** Focus on yourself, your journey and growth. Comparing yourself to others will only under-value and undermine your sense of worthiness and value. Your path and journey are uniquely planned just for you.

Self-esteem

Self-esteem is the overall opinion you have of yourself – your beliefs about yourself, how much you value and respect yourself, your evaluation of your strengths and abilities, and your character, qualities and core values and ideas.

Your self-esteem is rooted in your sense of self-worth and comes from your internal sense of self. It is primarily developed during childhood, from lived experiences and relationships.

Your beliefs about yourself, negative or positive, influence your level of self-esteem. If experiences and beliefs are positive, this leads to high self-esteem, reflected in fulfilling healthy relationships and lived experiences, and a belief about yourself that you are capable and can meet your needs. If experiences and beliefs are negative, this leads to low self-esteem, reflected in negative self-talk, lack of confidence, poor boundaries, a poor outlook, worry and doubt, negatively comparing yourself to others and looking for external validation.

To build your self-esteem means to cultivate a positive self-regard and opinion.

How to build your self-esteem

- **Acknowledge your strengths:** Create a self-esteem list of your strengths and abilities (see the following template). Keep adding to the list each day as you intentionally notice when you've demonstrated a strength, ability, quality or core value. Regularly review the list to reinforce your positive self-regard. (For more examples, see Chapter 10: Self-Love.)

- **Practise gratitude (Shukr):** Express gratitude for your strengths and abilities, as blessings and provisions from Allah (swt). (See Chapter 6 for ways to practise gratitude.)

- **Strengthen your relationship with Allah (swt):** Through prayer (Salah), remembrance of Allah (swt) (Dhikr) and supplication (Dua), you are building a strong connection between your core self and Allah (swt), which reinforces your core beliefs and values about yourself. There are many websites that list examples of dhikr and duas, where you can find and identify the ones that resonate with you, for you to practise as part of your daily remembrance.

- **Accept compliments:** Add to your self-esteem list the compliments and positive feedback you receive. Don't dismiss, belittle or minimize the positive feedback. Practise accepting and taking in compliments unconditionally, in the way they are given to you, with gratitude.

- **Stop your inner critic:** Challenge any negative or critical self-talk and replace with positive, affirming, empowering and compassionate thoughts. Speak to yourself with kindness and love. (See Chapter 8 for how to manage negative self-talk and self-sabotage behaviours.)

- **Boost your strengths and abilities:** Invest in personal growth and development to foster your positive beliefs about yourself. (See Chapter 16: Self-Growth to explore further.)

- **Journal your self-esteem journey:** Reflect on the following questions to help you connect and boost your self-esteem: What do you like about yourself? What skills, abilities and strengths have you acquired? What are your positive qualities, characteristics and core values? What have you achieved (big or small)? What challenges or difficulties have you overcome? Where have you shown robustness or resilience in your life? How do other people see you or describe you? What do other people like about you? What makes you a good friend? Fill in the following self-esteem list to validate your values. A full-size version is available to download. (See Chapter 12: Self-Values to identify your core values.)

SELF-ESTEEM LIST

Strengths

Abilities

Core Values

Qualities

Compliments and Positive Feedback

Self-confidence

Self-confidence is the self-belief and self-trust you have in your abilities and in being able to apply them to succeed, meet your potential and successfully handle any challenges you experience.

Self-confidence primarily starts internally through your own self-beliefs and self-trust, but it can be shaped and influenced by external feedback and validation. High self-confidence supports your initiative to act and work towards your goals, whereas low self-confidence stunts your personal growth, self-belief, decision making and motivation to work towards your goals.

Building self-confidence involves cultivating a belief and trust in your abilities.

How to build your self-confidence

- **Trust in Allah (swt) (Tawakkul):** Rely and trust in Allah (swt), knowing that He is always there for you, so you can handle any difficulties and challenges. Remind yourself that Allah (swt) is always there.

- **Seek knowledge:** Embrace new learning and growth. This could be a skill, hobby or sport, to boost your self-belief in navigating being outside of your comfort zone and doing something unfamiliar. Trust in Allah (swt) that He will guide you in your growth and development. (See Chapter 16 for support on how to set self-growth goals.)

- **Face your fears:** Practise being outside of your comfort zone, whether a new hobby, a new place or socially. Practise self-compassion that you are doing something unfamiliar, but each step is a win in building your self-trust.

- **Practise positive self-talk:** Speak positively and lovingly to yourself. Practise using the following affirmations to build a positive, believing inner voice, which believes in you and removes self-doubt. Remind yourself of the potential and abilities Allah (swt) has instilled and blessed upon you. Choose an affirmation that deeply resonates with you and speak this to yourself every day.

- **Take small steps:** Set a small goal, step or promise you can make and meet for yourself for the coming days. This will help build your self-trust when you follow through and do what you said you would do. (See Chapter 11 for ways to build your self-trust.)

- **Remember past achievements:** Remind yourself of all your past achievements, to boost your self-belief in your abilities. Keep a log or journal to record and track all your achievements (big and small). Always give yourself a pat on the back for each win and success, recognizing the abilities that Allah (swt) has blessed you with.

- **Stand with confidence:** Practise standing with confident body language. Head high and shoulders back. Take up your space. This will translate into feeling more confident internally.

To boost your self-worth, self-esteem and self-confidence, here are some positive affirmations to say to yourself daily. Choose ones that most resonate with you. Perhaps write them in your journal or on a sticky note to remind you of them and to build a daily practice of reciting them.

POSITIVE AFFIRMATIONS FOR SELF-WORTH, SELF-ESTEEM AND SELF-CONFIDENCE

I am good enough, as I am.
I am capable and able because Allah (swt) is my guide.
I rely on Allah (swt).
I stand firm and strong in who I am because Allah (swt) is my protector and guide.
I am human, just like everyone else.
I deserve love, care, kindness and respect unconditionally.
I trust in myself to do my best and be good enough.
I can be proud of what I achieve and have achieved.
I celebrate my successes.
I am grateful for all that Allah (swt) has blessed me with.
I am blessed with unique abilities and gifts by Allah (swt).
Making progress is more important than reaching for perfection.
I am learning from my experiences.
I am always growing.
I am on my unique journey.
I trust in Allah's (swt) plan for me.
My mistakes or failures do not define me or my worth.
Allah's (swt) mercy is greater than my flaws.

Add any more affirmations that come to mind. (For more positive affirmations, see the list of affirmations in Chapter 8.)

. . . .

. . . .

. . . .

REFLECTIONS

What are your reflections from this chapter?

. . . .

. . . .

. . . .

How would you rate your own self-worth, self-esteem and self-confidence (on a scale of 1–10, where 1 is lowest and 10 is highest)?

. . . .

. . . .

. . . .

Of those that you rated average or low, which actions or habits do you want to start practising or developing to build your self-worth, self-esteem and self-confidence?

. . . .

. . . .

. . . .

How do you currently communicate good or positive self-worth, self-esteem and self-confidence to yourself? What practices, words or actions communicate this?

. . . .

. . . .

. . . .

Are there any self-worth, self-esteem and self-confidence habits or practices that you are already doing but could be more intentional about? What would you do? How might you do that?

. . . .

. . . .

. . . .

Are there any self-growth goals you want to set for yourself, to support your development of self-worth, self-esteem or self-confidence?

. . . .

. . . .

. . . .

What self-worth, self-esteem and self-confidence actions or practices can you add to your self-care plan (see Chapter 4)?

. . . .

. . . .

. . . .

How can these practices and exercises further support your three relationship dimensions?

1. Relationship with Allah (swt):

. . . .

. . . .

2. Relationship with self:

. . . .

. . . .

3. Relationship with others:

. . . .

. . . .

CHAPTER 14

Self-Compassion

What is self-compassion?

Self-compassion is rooted in mercy (rahmah), forgiveness and self-awareness. It encourages you to balance striving for self-improvement with gentleness, recognizing human imperfection and Allah's (swt) infinite mercy. By reflecting on divine attributes, maintaining hope in Allah's (swt) forgiveness and nurturing your wellbeing, you can develop a compassionate approach to yourself.

This includes embracing the radical self-compassion approach, which is the powerful relational practice of deeply, unconditionally accepting yourself and embracing all parts of you with profound acceptance, love, care, kindness and understanding.

Self-compassion challenges internalized oppression, self-criticism, perfectionism, mistakes and flaws by transforming a negative relationship with yourself into one that is supportive, accepting, patient and kind. It moves you away from the individualistic, Western concept of self-care and towards anti-oppressive self-care and wellbeing that acknowledges and embraces all parts of you, your whole intersectional identity, your lived experiences and the context of your identity and experience within society. You offer understanding, kindness and love to yourself, especially during times of difficulty, challenge and struggle – times when it is hardest to offer yourself gentleness, yet when it is needed the most (Khan, 2023).

Radical self-compassion embraces your strengths, weaknesses, feelings and experiences without judgement. Rather, it allows you to honour your experience and perspective of what you are going through, how you are experiencing and responding, and how you are feeling.

Radical self-compassion brings you into the mind of our shared common humanity. No one is perfect, everyone makes mistakes and each of us experiences our own hardships. No one is immune. This supports you not to see your hardships, weaknesses or struggles in isolation or yourself as the only one going through difficulties.

Ways to build radical self-compassion
1. Start by reflecting and reminding
yourself of Allah's (swt) mercy

Begin and end your behaviours and actions with 'Bismillah-ir-Rahman-ir-Rahim' (In the Name of God – the Most Compassionate, Most Merciful, 1:1), which reminds and reconnects you to Allah's (swt) compassion. Recite and remind yourself of verses about Allah's (swt) mercy. (See Chapter 5: Relationship with Allah (swt) for examples.)

2. Practise self-kindness and gentleness

Treat yourself with the same genuine, unconditional kindness and gentleness that your faith encourages you to offer to others. Tell yourself: 'I am good enough as I am.'

Accept your flaws, mistakes and weaknesses as okay, natural and human parts of you, to be offered self-kindness, instead of harsh criticism, rejection and shaming yourself. Everyone experiences mistakes, growth and learning on their journey. Embracing these previously criticized and rejected parts of you means they become lessons and guidance for your future. Remind yourself: 'It is okay to make mistakes. It shows that I am learning and growing.' Use this as an affirmation to recite to yourself.

3. Let go of your inner critic

Replace your self-critical voice and narrative. Practise speaking to yourself with a kind, gentle and empathic voice, as you would to a loved one or as a friend would speak to you. When you find your inner critic speaking, take a self-compassion pause and reframe, to speak from your kind, gentle voice. Acknowledge any pain or suffering you are experiencing, recognize it as part of the human experience and speak to yourself with kindness instead of blame or shame.

Stop gaslighting yourself with self-blaming and shaming narratives, which position your feelings or experiences as wrong, such as 'I shouldn't feel like this', 'I should be able to get over it', 'I shouldn't let it bother me' or 'I don't deserve any good, success or happiness'. Notice how these self-blaming statements are about what you 'should' or 'shouldn't' be experiencing, about not meeting external expectations and feeling guilty. Instead, use your self-compassionate voice, to soothe yourself with forgiveness – 'I forgive myself, I am learning', 'I can make a mistake, I am not the mistake'. (See Chapters 8 and 13 for more on the inner critic and reframing negative self-talk.).

4. Practise compassionate self-talk

Practise and recite compassionate affirmations, quotes and mantras that create a self-compassion inner voice and dialogue, such as 'May I be at peace', 'I am worthy of love and kindness', 'I am deserving of care' or 'My feelings are welcomed and valued'. Use these affirmations when you notice your inner critic or self-criticism appearing. See below for examples of self-compassionate affirmations. (See Chapter 8 for additional positive affirmations.)

POSITIVE AFFIRMATIONS FOR SELF-COMPASSION

I show up for myself.

My efforts and rewards come from Allah (swt).

I choose to show myself compassion and acceptance.

I am worthy of love and kindness.

My self-worth comes from within.

I can work through any challenges or difficulties because Allah (swt) has given me the strength to overcome them.

I am doing the best with what I know right now.

I can have my needs met.

I set boundaries that are healthy for me and my relationships.

I strive to do and be my best for Allah's (swt) sake.

---

5. Seek forgiveness without self-blame and self-criticism

It is an act of self-compassion to seek forgiveness for yourself. Offer yourself the same forgiveness you would offer to others by seeking forgiveness and repentance, avoiding excessive guilt, blame, shame or despair, which will only keep you stuck in self-criticism without hope for forgiveness or release of this guilt. Seek repentance (Tawbah) sincerely, knowing that Allah (swt) loves those who turn to Him.

6. Cultivate self-awareness

Practise regular self-check-ins. Create a habit of checking in with yourself periodically throughout the day. Ask yourself: 'How am I feeling? (Name the feeling.) What do I need? What can I do for myself that is kind or gentle?'

Don't reject, try to fix or avoid any feelings that may come up. Instead, hold space for your feelings and observe them without judging them or labelling them as 'good' or 'bad'. Meet them with curiosity and compassion. Speak to them with care: 'I will be kind to this feeling', 'This feeling is telling me something important about my experience', 'I will honour and validate my feelings'. Ask yourself: What is this feeling telling me? Is it indicating what I need right now? Is this feeling telling me I need to work on something? (Use the Emotional Regulation Checklist in Chapter 21 to support this practice.)

7. Recognize your shared humanity

Remember that everyone makes mistakes and experiences failure, struggles and suffering. It is part of the human experience. You are not alone in experiencing these difficulties and challenges. Others will have similar experiences. Along with shared humanity, you can share compassion with yourself, as you would to others who are facing difficulties.

Positive affirmations can be extended to you and others together, such as 'We all go through challenges'.

8. Practise self-compassion writing

Write a letter to yourself, as if you were writing to a friend offering support, love and compassion. You could post the letter to yourself, so you receive it as if you were receiving a letter from a friend and/or keep it in your journal to re-read whenever you need to hear your own compassionate and kind words.

In your letter, acknowledge any struggle or difficulty you are experiencing with empathy and non-judgement. Express your understanding of the situation and your feelings towards it. Be gentle, hold and name your feelings and struggles, with no judgement, blame or guilt. Offer yourself empathy, concern, kindness and encouragement. Identify your strengths, core values and beliefs, which support you to be robust, strong and positive as you navigate any difficulty. Offer soothing, hopeful and comforting words, as you would to a friend or loved one. Offer a dua for ease and patience. Sign off with a positive affirmation and belief in yourself.

Reflect on the letter and use it to remind yourself of your strengths and abilities and to offer yourself compassion and comfort any time you need it.

9. Compassion as an act of charity to yourself

Charity (sadaqah) is as an act of compassion, and extending this to include yourself alongside others can mean investing in your own needs, self care and wellbeing. You are as deserving of your own compassion as everyone else who is also blessed to receive it. Use your self-care practice as part of your self-compassion relationship with yourself. (See Chapter 4 for self-care ideas and planning.)

10. Practise gratitude

Regularly focus on the blessings Allah (swt) has bestowed upon you in your life. Engage in a gratitude practice to express thankfulness and appreciation for the abundance and growth in your life, shifting your focus away from self-criticism and what is lacking to the abundance and blessings in your life. (See Chapter 6 to develop a gratitude practice.)

11. Practise balance in work and rest

Honour moderation in all areas of your life. It is emphasized to balance worship, work and rest. Listen to your needs without judgement or conditions. Rest is not earned. It is a necessary part of your wellbeing and relationship to yourself. (See Chapter 15: Rest and Burnout for the different types of rest you need.)

12. Practise healthy boundaries

Recognize where you are over-exerting or pushing yourself to the extent that you are not treating yourself with care and kindness. Practise setting boundaries that honour your needs, which respect your energy, time and effort, where you are considering your limits and capacity, and caring for yourself. Healthy boundaries are self-compassionate to your wellbeing and self-care needs. (See Chapter 22: Boundaries for further support.)

13. Establish a daily self-compassion routine

In the mornings, set an intention to be kind and compassionate to yourself. Think of three ways you can offer this to yourself (e.g. practise speaking kindly, having a break from your desk, having a quiet moment to yourself, eating lunch unhurriedly).

At the end of the day, reflect on three things you are grateful about yourself. It could be something you did that day, the way you responded to someone or a situation, or the way you showed up for yourself. It can be big or small. (See the daily gratitude journal template in Chapter 6 to support building a daily gratitude habit.)

By engaging in these techniques, you can cultivate deeper self-compassion for yourself, to support your wellbeing.

REFLECTIONS

What are your reflections from this chapter?

. . . .

. . . .

. . . .

How does your self-compassion show up? How do you show yourself compassion in your feelings, thoughts, intentions, words and actions?

. . . .

. . . .

. . . .

Which actions or habits do you want to start practising or developing to communicate self-compassion to yourself? What would you do? How might you do that?

. . . .

. . . .

. . . .

Are there any self-compassion habits that you are already practising but could be more intentional about? What would you do? How might you do that?

. . . .

. . . .

. . . .

Are there any self-growth goals you want to set for yourself, to support your development of self-compassion?

. . . .

. . . .

. . . .

What self-compassion actions or practices can you add to your self-care plan (see Chapter 4)?

. . . .

. . . .

. . . .

How can these practices and exercises further support your three relationship dimensions?

1. Relationship with Allah (swt):

. . . .

. . . .

2. Relationship with self:

. . . .

. . . .

3. Relationship with others:

. . . .

. . . .

CHAPTER 15

Rest and Burnout

Rest

We can often get caught up in the 'grind' or 'hustle' culture, in the glorification of being busy. It allows little or no time, space or permission for rest.

Yet for healthy, balanced wellbeing, rest is essential. Rest is more than just a momentary pause. Rest is a process of recharging yourself, instead of shutting off. Think of recharging your phone versus switching off your phone. Recharging rejuvenates your mind, body and soul for optimal wellbeing.

There are seven types of rest (see below) that you need, with each one supporting the different dimensions of your wellbeing and relationships:

- **Spiritual rest:** The time and opportunity to attune to your sense of purpose and nurture your connection to Allah (swt). This can be practised through activities such as prayer, practising gratitude, engaging in faith-community activities, book circles, study group or spending time in self-reflection connecting to your values and purpose.

- **Emotional rest:** The time and opportunity to sit with yourself without emotional pressures or judgement and connect to yourself authentically. This can be practised through activities such as journaling, self-reflection during time alone, being vulnerable and sharing how you are really feeling with a therapist or trusted friend.

- **Mental rest:** The time and opportunity to slow down your mind and thoughts, not being under constant mental strain and helping to manage and lighten your mental load. They can be practised through activities such as taking short breaks when working, engaging in mindfulness to be present in the moment, clearing or decluttering your mind by writing down anything on your mind or any worries you have and placing that mental load on a piece of paper to be contained, rather than carrying the burden and weight of those thoughts.

- **Social rest:** The time and opportunity to find a balance between engaging in nurturing relationships and limiting time with emotionally draining relationships. This can be practised through activities such as setting purposeful boundaries around time spent with others and time alone. What that split looks like between time with supportive friends and time alone is up to you, depending on what best serves your needs.

- **Physical rest:** The time and opportunity to rest and recover your physical body and energy. This can be practised through activities such as passive rest, sleeping, napping, resting the body fully, active rest activities (e.g. stretching, breathing exercises or leisurely walking).

- **Sensory rest:** The time and opportunity to reduce or remove any sensory stimuli or overwhelm. This can be practised through activities such as regular or scheduled breaks from screens and devices, switching off notifications, dimming or switching off lights, or spending time engaging in activities with no, minimal, reduced or additional sounds (i.e. having the TV or radio on in the background).

- **Creative rest:** The time and opportunity to engage in creative activities and think creatively. This could include visiting museums or galleries or any type of creative inspiration, such as being in nature and the outdoors, or it could be taking the time in pursue your own creative outlets or hobbies, such as painting, drawing, crafting or writing. Creative activities do not have to be directional, such as painting a picture; they could also include unstructured or emergent creative activities such as doodling, daydreaming or playing.

Engaging in all seven types of rest are supportive to our wellbeing. We may find that some types of rest are easier to engage in than others.

Here are some reflective questions to help support you to engage with resting and establish it as part of your self-care plan and wellbeing.

CREATIVE REST

time to engage in creative activities and think creatively

e.g. painting, drawing, crafting, going to museums or galleries

SENSORY REST

time to reduce or remove sensory stimuli or overwhelm

e.g. regular screen breaks, mute notifications, dimming or switching off lights

EMOTIONAL REST

time to sit and connect with yourself authentically and without emotional pressures

e.g. journaling, sharing your feelings with a therapist or trusted friend

SPIRITUAL REST

time to attune to your purpose and connection to Allah (swt)

e.g. prayer, gratitude, engaging in faith-community activities

PHYSICAL REST

time to rest and recover your physical body and energy

e.g. passive rest, sleeping, napping, stretching, breathing exercises

MENTAL REST

time to slow down your mind and not be under constant mental strain

e.g. taking short breaks, engaging in mindfulness to be present in the moment

SOCIAL REST

time to engage in nurturing relationships and limit emotionally draining ones

e.g. setting purposeful boundaries around time spent with others and time alone

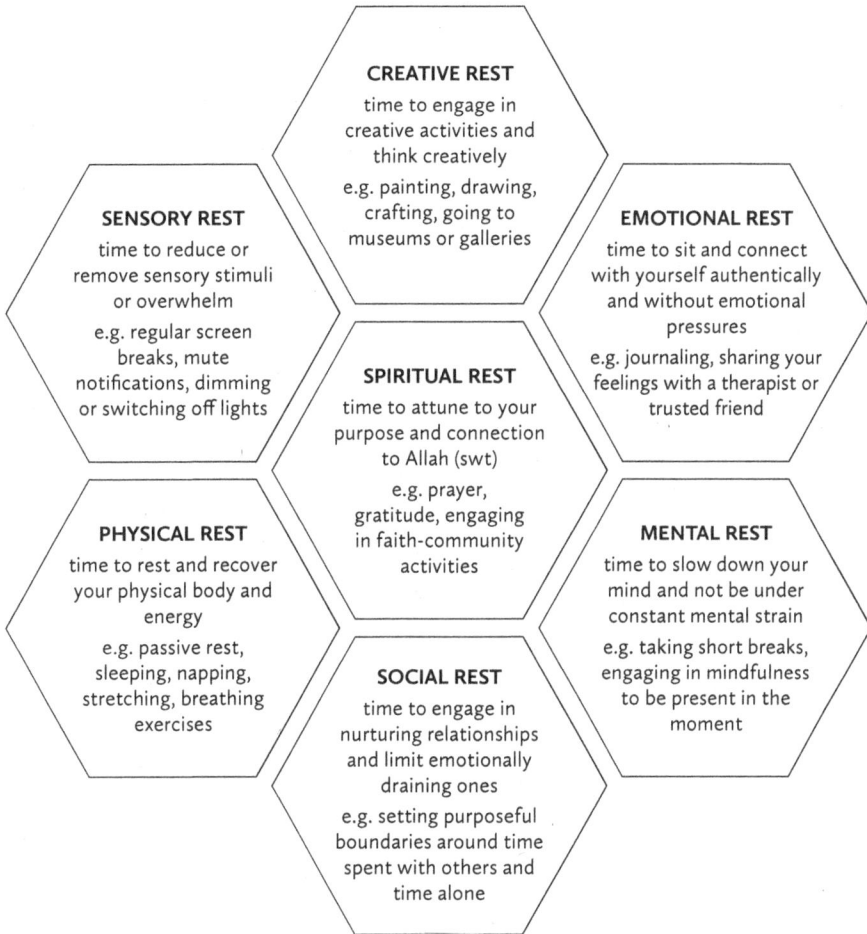

Seven types of rest

What is your relationship with rest?

. . . .

. . . .

. . . .

Are you comfortable with the seven types of rest? Which types are you comfortable with? Which types are you uncomfortable with?

. . . .

. . . .

. . . .

How do you currently practise rest? Which types of rest do you get? What do they look like in practice?

. . . .

. . . .

. . . .

Which types of rest are easier for you and why?

. . . .

. . . .

. . . .

Which types of rest are more challenging to you or don't allow yourself? Where do you struggle with rest?

. . . .

. . . .

. . . .

Which types of rest are you already practising? How can you build upon these types of rests? Could you do something more or something else?

. . . .

. . . .

. . . .

Which types of rest do you need to add into your self-care plan? What would these look like in practice?

. . . .

. . . .

. . . .

Having reflected on your experience of rest, perhaps you can identify the types of rest you need and how you can practise them. Add this to your types of rest plan here and to your self-care plan (in Chapter 4).

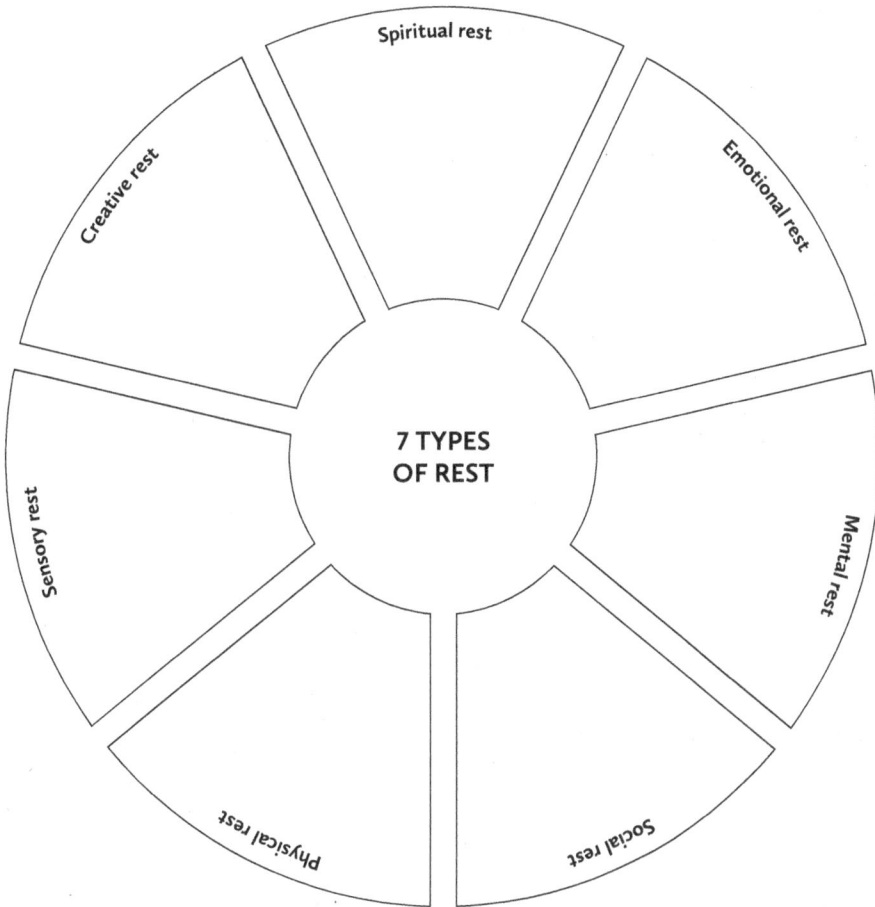

Spiritual rest
Emotional rest
Creative rest
Mental rest
Sensory rest
7 TYPES OF REST
Physical rest
Social rest

Types of rest plan

Bunout

Burnout is the condition of chronic mental, emotional and physical exhaustion, caused by the experience of prolonged and intense stress. It occurs when you feel overwhelmed, working beyond your capacity, having difficulty juggling demands and responsibilities, working long hours or high workloads, with poor work–personal life balance, poor sleep and/or quality of rest.

Burnout affects all aspects of your wellbeing, including your spiritual, emotional, physical and mental health, and impacts your relationships with yourself and others.

Key indicators of burnout include:

- **Emotional exhaustion:** Feeling emotionally drained and empty, feeling hopeless and dissatisfied and doubtful of improvements.

- **Physical exhaustion and symptoms:** Feeling physically drained, little to no energy even after rest or sleep, feeling 'wired' or 'little in the tank', poor quality of sleep, physical aches or pains, poor diet relying on caffeine or 'high-energy' processed foods.

- **Lack of accomplishment:** Feeling inadequate, incompetent or unfulfilled despite output or performance.

- **Lack of motivation and low performance:** Loss of enthusiasm and interest for what you previously enjoyed doing, struggling to concentrate, not working to your usual standards or productivity, lack of value or significance in your outputs.

- **Lack of meaning and purpose:** Loss of direction, disconnected from goals or purpose, feeling lost in life.

- **Impact on relationships:** Lack of social energy, feeling impatient or irritated, withdrawing from others.

- **Numbing coping strategies:** Coping by numbing out or shutting down through excessive actions (e.g. binge-watching TV, scrolling, over-eating, getting lost in distracting activities).

- **Lack of balance:** No time given to rest, hobbies and interests plus over-working and lack of breaks.

To identify if you may be experiencing burnout, here are some useful prompt questions to ask yourself.

Energy levels

- Am I feeling anxious, tense, stressed or emotionally exhausted?
- Am I feeling physically exhausted most of the time, even after sleeping and resting?
- Am I feeling mentally drained most of the time?

Physical symptoms

- Am I experiencing headaches, stomach issues or other physical issues?

- Am I experiencing insomnia, poor sleep, trouble falling asleep or staying asleep?
- Am I relying on caffeine, sugar or energy products to get through the day?

Coping mechanisms

- Am I using unhealthy coping mechanisms to deal with how I am feeling, such as over-eating, over-spending, substance use, external distractions?
- Am I avoiding tasks or responsibilities due to feeling stressed and overwhelmed?
- Am I distracting myself from tasks or responsibilities by numbing out via scrolling, binge-watching, other activities that take me away from the task at hand?

Motivation levels

- Have I lost motivation or interest in my tasks and responsibilities?
- Am I uninterested in starting or completing tasks?
- Am I struggling to focus or concentrate on tasks?
- Am I being unproductive or struggling to be productive to the level that I usually am?
- Do I feel that I'm not performing to my best?

Interest levels

- Am I feeling uninterested, detached or disconnected from my tasks or responsibilities?
- Am I feeling restless, resentful, fed-up, critical or negative towards my tasks or responsibilities?
- Do I feel that anything I do won't make a difference?

Success levels

- Am I feeling a lack of progress or accomplishment?
- Am I feeling inadequate, not good enough or not meeting expectations?
- Do I feel a sense of inability or incapability in my skills?

Social engagement levels

- Am I feeling socially exhausted or drained?

Finding time for myself

- Am I feeling that I have no energy for others?
- Am I withdrawing from others or isolating myself?
- Am I feeling irritated or impatient with others?

Having direction in life

- Do I feel that I don't have time for my interests and hobbies?
- Do I feel that I don't have the energy for interest in my hobbies?
- Do I feel guilty for taking breaks or rests and that I need to be spending the time on my work?
- Am I struggling to put in balanced and healthy work–personal life boundaries?

Feeling disconnected

- Am I feeling disconnected from my values, goals or sense of direction?
- Am I feeling misattuned to my purpose or meaning?
- Have I lost being in alignment with what matters to me?
- Am I questioning what I am doing in my life? Do I feel lost?
- Have I lost the feeling of purpose, value or alignment when doing my tasks?

Frequency of feelings

- Have I felt this way for a while, a long time, or is it a recent feeling?
- Am I feeling this way on a frequent, consistent daily basis?
- Have I been under a lot of stress or worry recently?
- Have I been pushing myself too hard or beyond my usual capacity?
- Have I struggled to find a good balance in my life?

If you answer 'yes' to any questions or recognize these signs in yourself, this may be an indication of feeling or building towards burnout. You may wish to engage in the following steps to support yourself to recover from burnout or prevent further burnout, as well as contacting your GP or medical professional for professional support.

Recovery from burnout addresses the key needs for rest and recovery, rediscovering your purpose, establishing boundaries and seeking support from others. It takes time, so you need to practice self-compassion throughout your recovery.

Ways to support yourself to recover from burnout

1. Acknowledge burnout

Recognizing your symptoms as burnout is the first step in recovery. Don't dismiss, minimize or push through the symptoms. Accept that this is burnout, and you need to treat your symptoms to enable recovery. Honour what you are experiencing and what you need to do for yourself as a necessity.

2. Practice self-compassion

Being compassionate to yourself and your experience is essential in taking care of yourself when you're burnt out. Treat yourself kindly and patiently. Take your time to know and meet your needs. Support yourself as you would recovering from a physical injury. (See Chapter 14 for ways to build a self-compassionate relationship with yourself.)

3. Prioritize rest and self-care

Ensure you are getting the different types of rest and self-care you need. Relaxing but also rejuvenating is part of recovery. Engage in stress-relieving activities. Do what feels nourishing, relaxing and gentle for you, such as quality sleep, a healthy diet, walking, gardening, reading, painting or light exercise. (See above for ideas for rest and Chapter 4 for self-care ideas.)

4. Take time off

Have a break from work or additional responsibilities where possible. Recovery requires rest and a break from feeling stretched and overwhelmed, beyond a day or weekend off. Book time off, if possible, to have time to prioritize your recovery and self-care.

5. Set boundaries

Practise saying 'no' to additional commitments at work or in your personal life. Create space for yourself and your recovery. Establish boundaries and bracket off time and space for your rest. Limit your outputs and spending energy externally. Use your time and space to offer your energy to yourself. (See Chapter 22 to support you in establishing boundaries.)

6. Reconnect with your values

Identifying your core values helps to rediscover your direction and purpose in life. What is important and a priority to you. It will help to redefine and align your values to your future goals and purpose. (See Chapter 12: Self-Values to help identify your core values.)

7. Reconnect with others

While burnout can leave you feeling socially drained, reconnecting with others who can hold space for you can bring about some comfort and decrease feelings of isolation and hopelessness. Plan for socializing activities that are not demanding and don't require high energy (e.g. meeting up for coffee or dinner or watching a movie together).

8. Don't overwhelm yourself further

Manage your recovery from burnout with small steps and changes. It would be easy to overwhelm and push yourself further by trying to do more or set unrealistic goals, but instead the opposite is needed. Do less. Find small habits you can implement that will be sustainable, manageable and won't over-extend you – try to get a regular bedtime routine, engage in easy, relaxing hobbies or light exercise.

9. Plan for prevention

As you recover from burnout, identify what may have caused your burnout. Was it a lack of boundaries? Overcommitting? Difficulty saying no? High workload?

Start to put measures in place to identify early warning signs and prevent you from experiencing burnout in the future. Are you feeling run-down or fatigued? Do you need to put better boundaries in? Look at your working hours or work–personal life balance? Identify core values and purpose? Do you need better time management? Extra support or help? Identify what you need to support your wellbeing and stress levels.

10. Seek professional support

Engage in support via a therapist or counsellor to explore the root causes and symptoms of your burnout, the impact on your wellbeing and ways to support you moving forward to prevent further bouts of burnout.

Remember that recovery takes time. Be patient with yourself. Listen to what you need and practise self-care compassionately to support your wellbeing.

REFLECTIONS

What are your reflections from this chapter?

. . . .

. . . .

. . . .

Have you experienced or are you experiencing burnout? What are the signs?

. . . .

. . . .

. . . .

Which actions or habits do you want to start practising to support your recovery from burnout? What would you do? How might you do that?

. . . .

. . . .

. . . .

Are there any habits that you are already practising to recover from or prevent burnout that you could be more intentional about? What would you do? How might you do that?

. . . .

. . . .

. . . .

Are there any self-growth goals you want to set for yourself to support your practice of rest or recovery/prevention from burnout?

. . . .

. . . .

. . . .

What recovery or prevention actions or practices can you add to your self-care plan (see Chapter 4)?

. . . .

. . . .

. . . .

How can these practices and exercises further support your three relationship dimensions?

1. Relationship with Allah (swt):

. . . .

. . . .

2. Relationship with self:

. . . .

. . . .

3. Relationship with others:

. . . .

. . . .

CHAPTER 16

Self-Growth

Self-growth and self-development are the mechanisms to improve yourself, your relationship with yourself and areas of your life. Self-growth focuses on your personal evolution, the process of developing self-awareness, insight and intelligence. Self-development focuses on the tangible steps to achieve your self-growth. The effect is for a better you, a fulfilled you, an authentic you in a state of healthy wellbeing.

Key practices to promote self-growth

1. Develop self-awareness

Practise daily reflection. Keep a journal to attune to, identify and understand your feelings, thoughts, values, beliefs and actions. This will support you in identifying your strengths and areas for growth. Reflect on each day's experience, how you've felt, what you've learnt and what you can do better the next day. Use the Emotional Regulation Daily Checklist in Chapter 21 to create a daily habit of checking in with your emotional self.

2. Set goals

Identify clear short-, medium- and long-term goals for a purposeful and meaningful life. Goals provide focus, direction and structure for success. See goals not just as the end outcome but as the learning and growth experienced throughout the process and journey itself. Set goals in the present and base them on what you do, how you want to be and how you show up every day for yourself and in relationships. Goals are not just materialistic, but means of growth and connection to yourself and the expression of you living your authentic self and life. Set goals as positive opportunities – as 'I want to (meet this goal)' and 'I get to' instead of the expectation or responsibility of 'I need to (meet this goal)' or 'I should'.

Fill in the self-growth tools and worksheets (at the end of the chapter) to help you to identify your goals and structure your self-growth process and progress for greater wellbeing.

3. Learn new skills

Embrace new learning (skills, knowledge, abilities) that will support your growth, open new opportunities, raise confidence and increase adaptability. Acquire new skills through a class, podcast, books, seminars or new hobby and interest. Perhaps invite friends to join you to support building your relationships with others. Make a list of interests, skills or hobbies you would like to try out.

4. Switch to a growth mindset

Reframe a negative outlook and inner critic of 'I can't' to a positive mindset of 'I can', I am trying' and 'I am learning'. This supports an abundant outlook filled with potential, opportunities and positive experiences, which will support a positive self-believing relationship with yourself. (See Chapter 8: Self-Sabotage and Inner Critic to support positive self-talk.)

5. Practise consistency

Establish a sustainable and realistic routine of growth habits. A routine supports consistency over time and a clear path of progress towards your goals. Start small with one habit at a time – read a chapter a day, go for a ten-minute walk in your lunchbreak, practise a gratitude exercise before sleeping. Create a routine that suits your timings and lifestyle. Use 'habit stacking', which is linking a new habit to an existing habit. The existing habit becomes the reminder or trigger to practise the new habit. For example, when you sit down at your desk or start work, state your intention for the day, listen to a podcast or audiobook on your commute, or have your gratitude journal by your bed to fill in before you go to sleep. Offer yourself lots of self-compassion, especially if you slip in your routine or don't complete a habit that day. Continue with your new habit and routine the next day. (See Chapter 14 on developing a self-compassion practice.)

6. Self-discipline

Honour your growth journey. Practise consistency and self-discipline towards your growth goals. Split your growth goals into manageable steps. Eliminate distractions to help focus on tasks. Create a timeline or practise a time management exercise to complete tasks, such as the Pomodoro Technique (focused work for 25 minutes followed by a five-minute break and repeat). Acknowledge your progress over time and recognize that your efforts are cumulative, supporting you to move closer to your goals.

7. Set boundaries

Set aside and protect time and space in your weekly schedule to invest in your goals and growth. Boundaries will help you to manage your energy and prevent burnout. Find time that works most effectively for you, such as early morning, late evening, weekends. (See Chapter 22 to help you establish healthy boundaries.)

8. Step outside your comfort zone

Growth happens outside of your comfort zone. Try new hobbies, interests or activities that will support your growth and goals. Embrace any mistakes or challenges as part of your learning and growth curve. Facing the unknown and unfamiliar boosts your confidence and belief in yourself, instead of being an excuse to stop trying.

9. Celebrate success

Acknowledge every step of progress and growth you make, no matter how big or small. See every step as getting closer to your goal. Assess your progress at the end of each week and recognize what achievements you've made, such as being consistent in a habit, completing a step, overcoming a difficulty or starting the next step.

10. Lean on your support circle

Have positive, supportive friends and family around you, or join a shared interest/goals group or community. Accept the support and encouragement they give you. Turn to them to ask for any help, support or encouragement you need. Have them as 'accountability' buddies to help you progress and move forward in your tasks and goals. Check in with them regularly with update and progress reports. (See Chapter 24 for ways to build your support circle.)

Nurturing your self-growth

Nurturing your self-growth daily involves small, intentional actions that focus on building a healthy relationship with yourself and working towards living authentically and fulfilled. This includes practising self-compassion, embracing new learning or setting goals which align with your core values.

EXAMPLES OF DAILY SELF-GROWTH HABITS

- Ten-minute morning and evening journaling
- Engaging in your hobby or interest
- List three things you are grateful for
- Send a message of appreciation to a loved one
- Acknowledge an achievement or win from the day

- Set your intention for the day
- Describe how you need to show up for yourself today
- Reflect on the day and how you want to show up for yourself tomorrow
- Listen to a podcast or audiobook
- Read a book which is comforting, inspiring or how you want to feel
- Watch an online seminar
- Take a photo of something that represents how you feel
- Go for a mindful walk
- Make decisions which align to your core values and beliefs

Self-growth tools and worksheets

Use the following self-growth tools and worksheets to support you to identify your wellbeing goals for self-growth. (These worksheets are also available to download.)

The wellbeing wheel

The wellbeing wheel below supports you to identify your fulfilment and satisfaction in each area of your wellbeing and which areas you would like to nurture and work on.

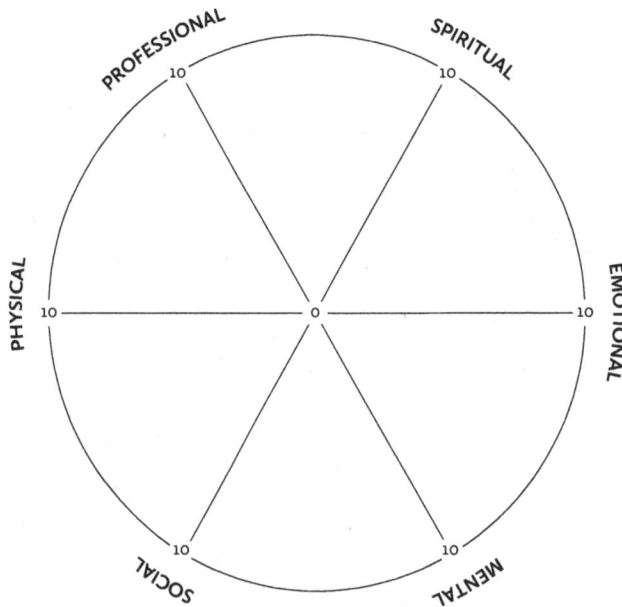

Wellbeing wheel

STEP 1. RATE EACH AREA

Reflect on each area of wellbeing. How are you currently feeling in that area of your life? How satisfied are you? Rate each area on a scale of 0-10, where 0 is completely dissatisfied and 10 is fully satisfied. Mark on the scales what rating you give each area. See below for the rating scale.

SATISFACTION RATING SCALE

0 – Completely dissatisfied
1 – Very dissatisfied
2 – Dissatisfied
3 – Somewhat dissatisfied
4 – Neutral
5 – Somewhat satisfied
6 – Satisfied
7 – Very satisfied
8 – Highly satisfied
9 – Extremely satisfied
10 – Fully satisfied

STEP 2. REFLECT ON YOUR SCALING

Look at the different ratings you have given. How do you feel about the ratings you've given? What comes up for you when you notice the rating given? What thoughts or reflections do you have? Support your feelings, thoughts and reflections with self-compassion if you find yourself with any negative self-talk or critical voice.

. . . .

. . . .

. . . .

. . . .

. . . .

. . . .

. . . .

Of the areas rated 8–10, what can you continue to do, to ensure they remain at 8–10? What would that look like? What would you be doing more or less of?

. . . .

. . . .

. . . .

. . . .

. . . .

Of the areas rated 5–7, what can you do to support these areas and move them up to 8–10? What would you be doing? What would that look like?

. . . .

. . . .

. . . .

. . . .

. . . .

Of the areas rated 1–4, why do you think these areas are lower than the others? What is missing or not happening that means you don't feel satisfied in these areas? What could you do to improve your satisfaction in any of these areas? What would you be doing? What would that look like?

. . . .

. . . .

. . . .

. . . .

. . . .

Wellbeing goal-setting worksheet

Having identified areas for growth and nurturing in your self-care and wellbeing, you can begin to create an intentional plan of how to identify, set and meet your wellbeing goal(s). Using the Wellbeing Goal Setting worksheet, answer the questions listed to create a self-growth plan to invest and nurture your underrated wellbeing areas.

WELLBEING GOAL SETTING

1. What areas in my wellbeing do I want to focus on for self-growth? (*e.g. spiritual, emotional, mental or physical wellbeing, practise types of rest, recover from burnout, set boundaries, practise self-care*)

....

....

2. What specific goal do I want to achieve?

....

....

3. Why is this goal important to me?

....

....

4. What steps will I take to achieve this goal?

....

....

Specific: What is my goal in one sentence? What do I want to accomplish?

....

Measurable: How will I know I've met my goal?

....

Achievable: What actions do I need to take to complete this goal?

....

Relevant: Why is achieving this goal important to me? What value will reaching my goal give me?

....

Time: When will I (need to) reach my goal?

....

5. What barriers or challenges might I face and how will I overcome them?

....

....

6. How will I know that I am progressing towards my goal? What will I notice, feel or experience?

....

....

Wellbeing goals tracker

Having created a plan to meet a wellbeing goal, which you can now action, use the Wellbeing Goals Tracker below to monitor your goal progress. Remember to practice self-compassion and self-love as you start your self-growth and discovery journey towards this goal. Work with your self-esteem, self-confidence and self-worth to overcome any challenges, difficulties or internal inner critics and negative self-talk. Look to Chapter 8 on self-sabotage for practices to overcome any negativity that you find along your path, whether that be your own sabotaging actions, behaviours or inner dialogue and beliefs.

Wellbeing goals tracker

Goal:				
Action/steps	**Target date**	**Progress**	**Notes**	**Reflections**

Monthly progress review

Along any goal journey and process, track your progress using the monthly progress review here to help you identify what your successes, challenges and lessons learnt have been. This will support you to understand the direction of travel you have taken and are taking towards your goal, what progress you've made and what you may need to continue in order to succeed and reach your goal.

MONTHLY PROGRESS REVIEW

1. What progress have you made over this past month? What achievements or successes have you experienced?

....

....

....

2. What challenges have you experienced? How did you overcome them?

....

....

....

3. Are your goals still accurate? Do you need to adjust them in any way?

....

....

....

4. What do you need to do this coming month to stay on track?

....

....

....

5. What signs or changes have you noticed in your wellbeing, feelings, thoughts or actions that reflect your self-growth?

....

....

....

6. How can you motivate yourself, or what do you need, to keep progressing in your goals and self-growth?

....

....

....

....

Use these worksheets and trackers to identify, structure and manage your self-growth goals and process. Keep reviewing as you go along to monitor your progress, celebrate your achievements and successes, and reflect on the learning and growth during the process itself and not just once the goal has been achieved.

REFLECTIONS

What are your reflections from this chapter?

. . . .

. . . .

. . . .

Have you identified any areas for self-growth?

. . . .

. . . .

. . . .

Which actions or habits do you want to start practising to support your self-growth? What would you do? How might you do that?

. . . .

. . . .

. . . .

Are there any self-growth areas, habits or practices that you are already doing but could be more intentional about? Could this be a new goal to invest in and commit to? What would you do? How might you do that?

. . . .

. . . .

. . . .

Are there any self-growth goals you want to set for yourself?

. . . .

. . . .

. . . .

What self-growth actions or practices can you add to your self-care plan (see Chapter 4)?

. . . .

. . . .

. . . .

How can these practices and exercises further support your three relationship dimensions?

1. Relationship with Allah (swt):

. . . .

. . . .

2. Relationship with self:

. . . .

. . . .

3. Relationship with others:

. . . .

. . . .

CHAPTER 17

Emotions

What are emotions?

Emotions are complex psychological states that involve a range of feelings, thoughts and behaviours. They are an integral part of the human experience, created by Allah (swt) as a guide, a test, a way to connect to yourself, others and Allah (swt), and influence how you experience and respond to the world around you.

Emotions typically arise in response to internal or external stimuli. Emotions consist of the internal feeling, physiological response and external response or outward behaviour in response to the emotion. It is encouraged to understand and process your emotions to support your wellbeing and emotional health.

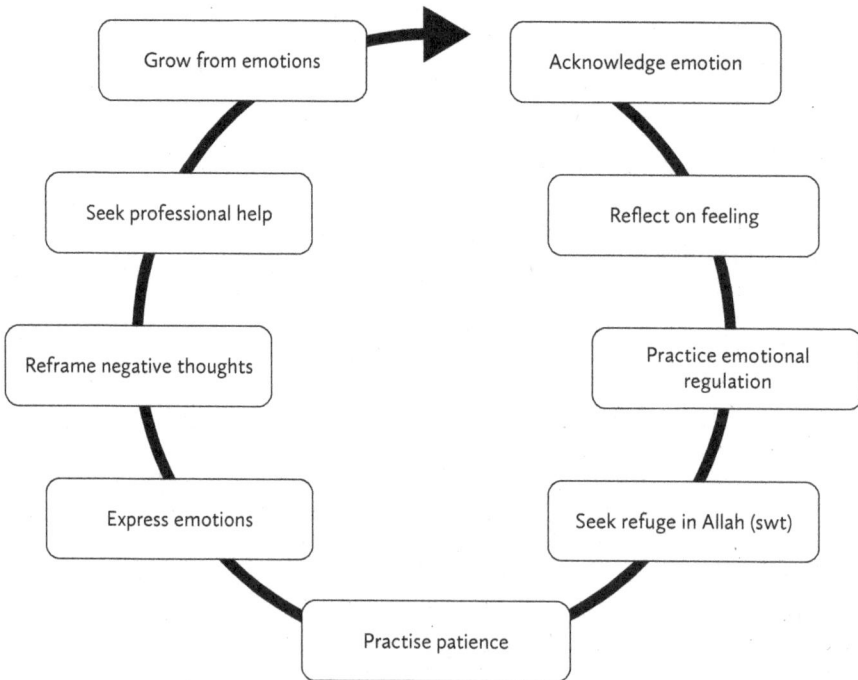

Process emotions flowchart

How to process emotions

1. Acknowledge the emotion

Identify the emotion you are feeling. Try not to ignore or push away the feeling. Name the feeling: 'I am feeling...' Don't label it as 'good' or 'bad'. Practise self-compassion to be with the feeling without judgement. It may feel uncomfortable, but it is necessary to process your feelings. Use the feelings wheel below to help you identify your feeling and attune yourself to what you are feeling. This is especially important if you have learnt to neglect, push away or avoid feelings through self-abandonment habits.

Feelings wheel

2. Reflect on the feeling

Ask yourself: What might have caused the emotion? You may have experienced a particular experience, interaction or thought. Notice what additional feelings you may have alongside or beneath the initial emotion. Often, deeper feelings sit beneath your first feeling, – for example, underneath anger could be feelings of fear, sadness, loss or grief. Identify if there is a root cause to your emotions and therefore look to support that root feeling.

3. Practise emotional regulation

Practise breathing exercises and grounding techniques to regulate your emotions, to bring you back into feeling grounded and emotionally stable in yourself. (See Chapter 21: Emotional Regulation for exercises and techniques.)

4. Seek refuge in Allah (swt)

Turn to Allah (swt) in prayer (salah) and supplication (dua) for relief, comfort and peace, especially if you are feeling overwhelmed or filled with emotions. There are many websites and apps that offer dua/supplication recommendations based on how you are feeling and to support specific feelings and emotions. Please find those that resonate with you, to use and recite when you need to.

5. Practise patience (sabr)

Recognize the test in managing your emotions. Endure hardships with patience and self-control. This does not mean ignoring, dismissing, minimizing or pushing away your emotions, but rather managing and looking after them with patience and self-compassion.

6. Express your emotions

Use creative outlets to express how you are feeling, Journaling helps to clarify feelings, find insights and process your feelings. Use creative methods such as art, painting, doodling or photography to release and express feelings nonverbally. Physical exercise or movement – for example, walking, running, going to the gym, swimming – releases stored-up emotions and energy somatically. (See Chapter 10 for a daily wellbeing journal template.)

7. Reframe negative thoughts

Challenge the negative thoughts or beliefs that you connect to your feelings, which might be keeping you stuck or spiralling in your emotions. Replace with positive thoughts to offer a self-compassionate, supportive, kind inner dialogue and beliefs to your emotions. (See Chapters 8 and 14 on self-sabotage and self-compassion to find ways to reframe negative thoughts.)

8. Seek professional help

When feeling emotionally overwhelmed or dysregulated for a long period of time or struggling to process emotions on your own, seek help with a therapist or counsellor. This will offer you a space to process your emotions, find root causes and provide ways to emotionally regulate yourself.

If you find yourself identifying, uncovering or releasing emotional pain, distress or trauma from past experiences, relationships or events that are impacting your current emotional state or daily life experience, it is strongly recommended to seek professional help to support you to process this deeper work for emotional healing.

9. Grow from your emotions

Learning and finding insights from your emotions supports your self-growth and development. Reflect on what teachings your emotions are communicating to you as they are signals to what in yourself needs attention. If familiar emotions are triggered by behaviours or situations, start to look at what you can address and change to support emotional healing and emotional regulation within yourself. (See Chapter 16 for how to set goals for your self-growth.)

To guide you through these steps and to support processing your emotions, use the following emotions check-in worksheet.

EMOTIONS CHECK-IN

Identify your emotion:

. . . .

What might have caused this emotion?

. . . .

What additional feelings might you be feeling alongside or beneath the initial emotion?

. . . .

Is there a root cause to your emotions and feelings?

. . . .

What breathing exercise or grounding technique can you use to regulate yourself?

. . . .

What spiritual practice can you turn to (prayer, supplication or recitation)?

. . . .

What can you do to express your emotions and feelings creatively?

. . . .

Are there any negative thoughts or beliefs that accompany these feelings?

. . . .

What positive thoughts or beliefs can you replace them with instead?

. . . .

What is your emotion communicating to you? What can you learn from this emotion?

. . . .

What else do you need to do to constructively respond to your emotion?

. . . .

What do you need to do for your self-care as you are processing this emotion?

. . . .

Recognize that emotions are a natural, intentional and meaningful part of your everyday life. They are not to be managed away, to feel numb or neutral. Emotions are at the heart of your relationship with Allah (swt), with yourself and with others. Looking after your emotions, to support emotional maturity, regulation, availability and safety, serves your emotional self-care and wellbeing for healthy relationships and optimal wellbeing. (See Chapters 18, 21, 26 and 27 for more information on emotional maturity, regulation, availability and safety.)

REFLECTIONS

What are your reflections from this chapter?

. . . .

. . . .

. . . .

How do you process your emotions or what do you do to your emotions?

. . . .

. . . .

. . . .

How can you better process your emotions? What can you do to support yourself to sit with and process your emotions? What would you do? How might you do that?

. . . .

. . . .

. . . .

Are there any habits or practices that you are already doing to process your emotions that you could be more intentional about? Could this be a new goal to invest in and commit to? What would you do? How might you do that?

. . . .

. . . .

. . . .

Are there any self-growth goals you want to set for yourself, to support your development of processing emotions?

. . . .

. . . .

. . . .

What actions or practices can you add to your self-care plan (see Chapter 4)?

. . . .

. . . .

. . . .

How can these practices and exercises further support your three relationship dimensions?

1. Relationship with Allah (swt):

. . . .

. . . .

2. Relationship with self:

. . . .

. . . .

3. Relationship with others:

. . . .

. . . .

CHAPTER 18

Emotional Maturity

What is emotional maturity?

Emotional maturity is your ability to manage and respond to your emotions in a healthy, regulated, self-aware and constructive manner, while simultaneously holding other people's emotions as separate from yours with respect and understanding.

Emotional maturity reflects your emotional self-growth, self-awareness and ability to respond to others and situations with emotional robustness, clarity and reflexivity.

Key aspects of emotional maturity

- **Self-awareness:** You have insight of what your emotions are, how they affect your thoughts, behaviours and responses, and why you are feeling that emotion. You can pause, reflect and respond to your emotions instead of reacting to them. Develop your self-awareness by regularly reflecting on your feelings, thoughts, actions and emotional responses. Use journaling techniques or take pauses for moments of reflection to check in with your emotions and emotional responses. Use the emotions check-in worksheet in Chapter 17 to support this process. (See also Chapter 10 for a daily wellbeing journal template.)

- **Emotional regulation:** You can manage your emotions effectively and bring yourself into an emotionally balanced state. You can feel your emotions without them overwhelming or controlling you and can respond to them appropriately and thoughtfully, not reactively or impulsively. (See Chapter 21 for emotional regulation techniques.)

- **Empathy:** You can empathize with other people's feelings and understand and respect how someone else may be feeling. You can consider other people's perspectives, while simultaneously respecting and honouring your own feelings. Develop your empathy by practising active listening to others, without judgement, interruptions or a need to speak, but instead by holding space for them. Ask questions to develop your understanding of them without the need to find a solution or give advice. Try to understand from their perspective, even if it doesn't match your own.

- **Forgiveness:** You can let go and forgive others for past hurts, without holding resentment or negativity. You recognize that holding on to resentment only hurts and blackens your own heart. You focus on the present and future, recognizing what is more important for your own future and blessings.

- **Robustness:** You can navigate and adapt to life's changes and challenges without becoming overwhelmed. You see changes as opportunities for growth and learning. Build your robustness by intentionally and actively looking for the growth, learning and lessons from any setback or difficulty. Use positive self-talk or affirmations to honour your growth through these challenges. (See Chapter 8 on self-sabotage for how to challenge negative self-talk and Chapter 20 on building emotional robustness.)

- **Responsibility:** You take full responsibility and accountability for your emotions and how you respond and manage them. You do not project, blame or deflect responsibility on to anyone else. Build your responsibility by acknowledging the impact of your words, actions and emotional responses on others, and speaking up, apologizing or explaining when needed, if any hurt or rupture has been caused in your relationships and communications.

- **Healthy boundaries:** You can set healthy boundaries in relationships with yourself and others, to support your wellbeing. You can develop setting healthy boundaries by recognizing where, when and how to say 'no', and learning that boundaries are a sign of healthy respect to you and others. (See Chapter 22 for how to set healthy boundaries.)

- **Clear communication:** You communicate clearly, openly and honestly, even in a difficult conversation or conflict. You avoid using passive-aggressive, destructive or disrespectful behaviour or language to cause ruptures in your relationships. You aim for productive and meaningful conversations, which foster nurturing and reparative relationships. Build clear communication skills by practising open, honest conversations, where you can share appreciation, express gratitude and build connections with others.

Emotional maturity results in deeper self-awareness, healthier relationships, self-growth, increased confidence and security in your sense of self for a more balanced wellbeing and fulfilled life. Emotional maturity is an ongoing emerging process throughout life to practise and build, to strengthen your ability to manage your emotions and emotional responses.

REFLECTIONS

What are your reflections from this chapter?

. . . .

. . . .

. . . .

How do you demonstrate emotional maturity in your words, actions and relationships? How do you recognize emotional maturity in yourself?

. . . .

. . . .

. . . .

Which emotionally mature actions or habits do you want to start practising or developing? What practices can you begin to act on, to support your development? What would you do? How might you do that?

. . . .

. . . .

. . . .

Are there any emotionally mature actions, behaviours or habits that you are already practising but could be more intentional about? What would you do? How might you do that?

. . . .

. . . .

. . . .

Are there any self-growth goals you want to set for yourself, to support your development of emotional maturity?

. . . .

. . . .

. . . .

What emotionally mature actions or practices can you add to your self-care plan (see Chapter 4)?

. . . .

. . . .

. . . .

How can these practices and exercises further support your three relationship dimensions?

1. Relationship with Allah (swt):

. . . .

. . . .

2. Relationship with self:

. . . .

. . . .

3. Relationship with others:

. . . .

. . . .

CHAPTER 19

Emotional Needs

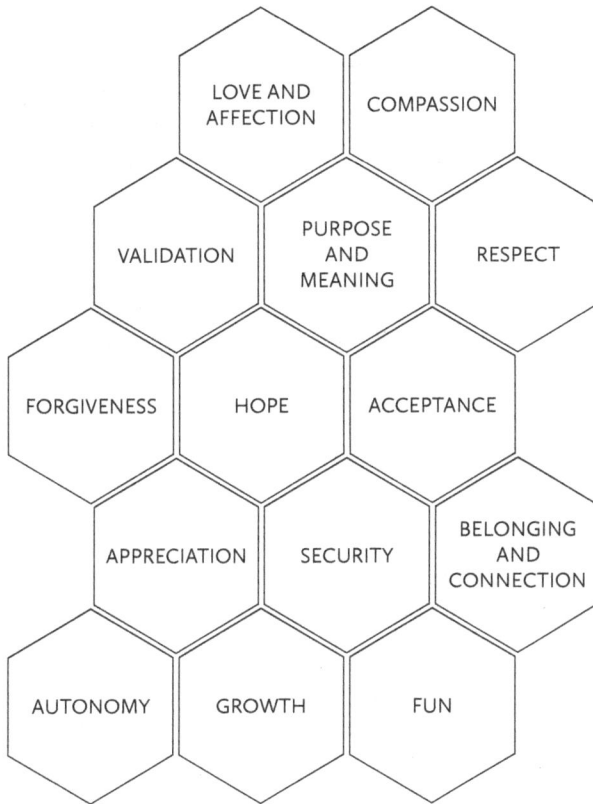

Emotional needs

What are emotional needs?

Your emotional needs are part of your human nature, created by Allah (swt) to support and nurture a balanced emotional life of inner peace, robustness and contentment. They are essential feelings and emotional experiences, which contribute to your wellbeing, quality of relationships and sense of self, to foster a balanced, fulfilled life. Your emotional needs align with core beliefs, values and principles of being the 'best' person you can be in your character, personality, intentions and interactions for healthy relationships, to create positive and fulfilling life experiences and relationships for yourself, which are rooted in your faith.

When your emotional needs are met and fulfilled, you feel secure, valued and connected. You offer yourself the ability to feel empowered in your life and connected in your relationships with yourself, with others and with Allah (swt), which support healthier relationships and a stronger sense of self.

By offering and meeting your emotional needs with yourself first, you build a balanced, fulfilled emotional relationship with yourself, which can be mirrored in your relationships with others. If emotional needs become unmet, it leads to feeling and experiencing dissatisfaction, stress, anxiety, loneliness, emptiness and isolation in life, which are significant negative impacts on all areas of your wellbeing.

Your emotional needs are:

- **Love and affection:** You feel love and loved, with love being expressed by you and to you through affection, gentleness and compassion. You can feel and receive love and affection shown to you, through love languages that feel fulfilling and enriching to you. (See Chapter 10: Self-Love for more on self-love languages.)

- **Compassion:** You feel and experience self-compassion and empathy towards your feelings and experiences, and you experience compassion from others towards you too. You and others can offer empathy and understanding to your experiences, without judgement, criticism or blame, which are held with compassion, love and kindness. (See Chapter 14 on ways to nurture your self-compassion.)

- **Validation:** You feel your feelings, thoughts, opinions, beliefs and experiences are seen, heard and acknowledged as valid and real by yourself and others, and are accepted as your 'truth' and lived experience, which supports your self-worth and self-value.

- **Purpose and meaning:** You feel your sense of purpose every day or in your daily routine, habits and behaviours. You feel engaged in learning, self-growth and development in your life. You feel your life's purpose has deep meaning to you, which is aligned with your faith and beliefs. You feel you are cultivating and experiencing a fulfilled life because it is aligned with your faith and its guidance for a purposeful and meaningful life.

- **Respect:** You feel respected and valued by others, and your dignity is honoured to support your own self-respect, integrity and modesty, without arrogance or pride, as a creation of Allah (swt). Your self-worth and self-value are supported by the respect and dignity shown to you.

- **Forgiveness:** You feel and experience opportunity for forgiveness in your relationships and can work towards repairing relationships if any rupture or conflict occurs. Reconciliations and repairs in your relationships are available and offered to you. You experience genuine forgiveness from others, without your mistakes or any grudges being held on to. Your relationships are looked after to support community, social and relational harmony and happiness.

- **Hope:** You feel hopeful, optimistic and robust as you go about your everyday life, especially when you are experiencing difficult times, challenges or hardships. You have a hopeful and optimistic outlook on life and look towards a hopeful future, as you are motivated to move forward with positive intentions and actions. You place your trust and faith in Allah's (swt) plans for you and for His mercy, as you hold on to hope in your life and what is planned for you. This supports you to build emotional robustness and perseverance as you navigate your daily life and any challenges.

- **Acceptance:** You feel accepted for your full authentic self, including your imperfections and flaws, without any judgement or pressure to be someone else or to change who you are or any part of you. This supports you to feel safe or safe enough and to have a sense of belonging, in relationships and spaces.

- **Appreciation:** You feel and experience being appreciated and valued for who you are, for your values and qualities, and for the efforts you make to help or support others. You feel that what you offer and bring to relationships, work and/or tasks is noticed, seen and valued by others, who share with you their appreciation of what you bring.

- **Security:** You feel emotionally safe or safe enough, secure and trusting in your relationships and home environment, to experience healthy and stable relationships and a safe home environment, which brings about peace of mind and a sense of calm for you.

- **Belonging and connection:** You are part of a community (family, group, friends, collective identity, social or special interest group) that you feel you belong and are emotionally connected to, where you feel accepted and can access support when you need it, and where you don't feel alone. You feel part of a greater or wider collective identity that you belong to and identify with, beyond your individual sense of self as an 'I', and can identify with a collective 'we' or 'us'.

- **Autonomy:** You feel capable and trustworthy to make decisions for yourself. You feel a degree of choice and control in your life to make choices through your own free will. This supports your self-confidence and self-esteem to trust and rely on yourself to make the best choices and decisions for yourself and contribute towards your self-growth.

- **Growth:** You feel you can set, work towards and achieve goals. You feel capable of overcoming challenges and any setbacks on the path towards reaching your goals. You seek continual improvement for yourself through self-growth and personal development practices and habits. You can feel and acknowledge a sense of accomplishment and self-growth in your progress and journey towards your goals. (See Chapter 16: Self-Growth for more.)

- **Fun:** You feel and experience joy, playfulness and excitement. You make time for fun and enjoyable activities and experiences, without any guilt or shame or feeling that it is 'childish'. Instead, you can acknowledge your need for fun, no matter your age, and feel able to relax and enjoy having fun, be spontaneous and be in the moment, either on your own or with others.

Take some time to reflect on these emotional needs.

How do you experience them in your life? Do you feel your emotional needs are met?

. . . .

. . . .

. . . .

Using the rating scale (below), how are you currently feeling about your experience of each emotional need? How satisfactorily do you feel these needs are met? Rate each need on a scale of 0–10, where 0 is completely dissatisfied and 10 is fully satisfied. Mark below what rating you give each emotional need.

SATISFACTION RATING SCALE

0 – Completely dissatisfied
1 – Very dissatisfied
2 – Dissatisfied
3 – Somewhat dissatisfied
4 – Neutral
5 – Somewhat satisfied
6 – Satisfied
7 – Very satisfied
8 – Highly satisfied
9 – Extremely satisfied
10 – Fully satisfied

Love and affection: . . . .

Compassion: . . . .

Validation: . . . .

Purpose and meaning: . . . .

Respect: . . . .

Forgiveness: . . . .

Hope: . . . .

Acceptance: . . . .

Appreciation: . . . .

Security: . . . .

Belonging and connection: . . . .

Autonomy: . . . .

Growth: . . . .

Fun: . . . .

Reflect on your scaling: Look at the different ratings you have given.

Ask yourself: How do you feel about the ratings you've given? What comes up for you when you notice the rating given? What thoughts or reflections do you have? Support your feelings, thoughts and reflections with self-compassion if you find yourself with any negative self-talk or critical voice.

....

....

To meet your emotional needs, the first place to start is with yourself. How can you offer these needs to yourself? Identify what you can do to build a relationship with yourself in which you are meeting your emotional needs.

....

....

Of the emotional needs rated 8–10, what can you continue to do to ensure they remain at 8–10? What would that look like? What would you be doing more or less of?

....

....

Of the emotional needs rated 5–7, what can you do to support these needs to be met and move them up to 8–10? What would you be doing? What would that look like?

....

....

Of the emotional needs rated 1–4, why do you think these needs are lower than the others? What is missing or not happening to feel satisfied in these needs being met? What could you do to improve your satisfaction with any of these needs? What would you be doing? What would that look like?

....

....

....

How to meet your emotional needs

Your relationship with yourself becomes the mirror to nurture your relationship with others and for others to mirror meeting your needs. Fill in the worksheet below to identify the ways in which you can start to meet your emotional needs and begin to put them into practice using the goal-setting strategy illustrated in Chapter 16.

Meeting my emotional needs

Emotional need	Practices to meet this need	How can you meet this need?
Love and affection	Express love to yourself. Use your primary love languages to show love.	
Compassion	Show kindness towards yourself. Don't self-criticize or blame for any mistakes.	
Validation	Identify how you feel and validate your feelings as real. Journal your daily reflections, feelings and thoughts.	
Purpose and meaning	Lean into your faith. Re-align with your beliefs. Affirm your intentions. Identify how you want to grow in life and align with your values.	
Respect	Respect yourself through positive self-talk. Set healthy boundaries. Practise integrity in your words and interactions. Set intentions of your values showing up in your relationships.	
Forgiveness	Let go of any blame or guilt you feel for past mistakes. Identify resentments you need to let go of. Pray for forgiveness. Apologize to those who you need to say sorry to.	
Hope	Practise positive self-talk for a positive outlook. Identify hopeful and optimistic affirmations you can repeat to yourself daily.	
Acceptance	Practise accepting yourself as you are. Recognize your worth. Identify all parts of you without judgement.	

cont.

Emotional need	Practices to meet this need	How can you meet this need?
Appreciation	Practise appreciating yourself through gratitude. Note down daily what you are grateful for about yourself, how you show up and what you do for yourself.	
Security	Identify ways you feel emotionally safe in the areas of your life. Practise reciting that you place your trust in Allah's (swt) plan, as a daily affirmation and intention.	
Belonging and connection	Spend quality time with loved ones. Invest time in new friendships and groups. Identify those who feel safe for you to go to when you need help. Identify your social circle and your communities.	
Autonomy	Recognize and trust the choices and decisions you make for yourself. Appreciate that you are looking out for yourself and what is best for you.	
Growth	Set goals for yourself, track your progress and celebrate successes.	
Fun	Engage in activities and hobbies you enjoy. Experiment with new activities. Invite friends or family to go to fun activities with you. Identify what your interests are and see how you can engage in those interests (e.g. classes, groups, meet-ups, social events).	

Having identified ways in which you can start to meet your emotional needs, you may discover, as you start to practise them, that there are more ways your needs are being met or can be met. Fill in the following emotional needs plan as you discover and add more ways to how your emotional needs can be met, as part of your self-care and wellbeing plan.

EMOTIONAL NEEDS PLAN

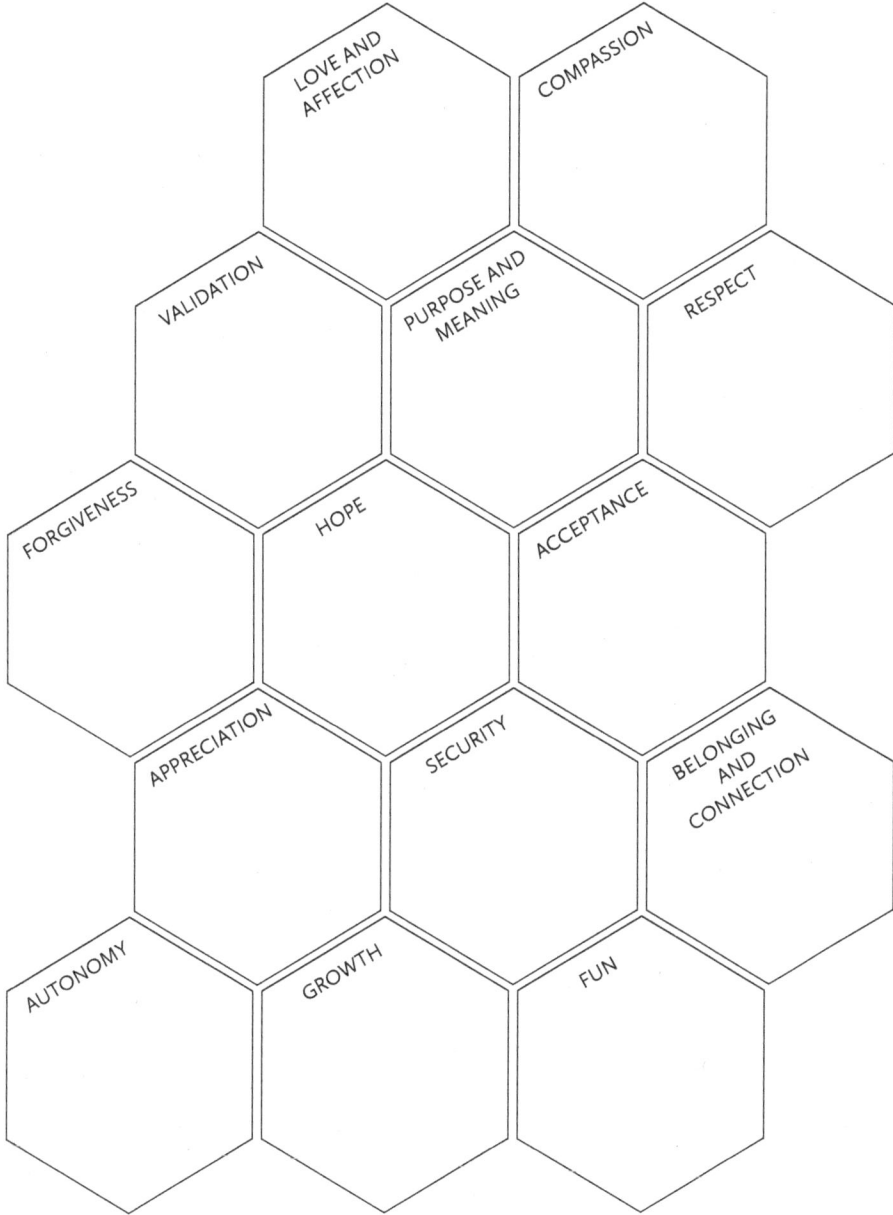

LOVE AND AFFECTION

COMPASSION

VALIDATION

PURPOSE AND MEANING

RESPECT

FORGIVENESS

HOPE

ACCEPTANCE

APPRECIATION

SECURITY

BELONGING AND CONNECTION

AUTONOMY

GROWTH

FUN

Honouring and meeting your emotional needs, in a manner aligned with faith, are important to support and nurture a balanced emotional state and wellbeing, your relationship with Allah (swt), your relationship with yourself and your relationship with others.

REFLECTIONS

What are your reflections from this chapter?

. . . .

. . . .

. . . .

How do you feel about your emotional needs being met or not being met?

. . . .

. . . .

. . . .

To meet your emotional needs, what practices can you begin to act on? What might be your first steps? What would you do? How might you do that?

. . . .

. . . .

. . . .

Are there any actions, behaviours or habits that you are already practising but could be more intentional about, to meet your emotional needs more satisfactorily? What would you do? How might you do that?

. . . .

. . . .

. . . .

Are there any self-growth goals you want to set for yourself, to support meeting your emotional needs?

. . . .

. . . .

. . . .

What emotional needs actions or practices can you add to your self-care plan (see Chapter 4)?

. . . .

. . . .

. . . .

How can these practices and exercises further support your three relationship dimensions?

1. Relationship with Allah (swt):

. . . .

. . . .

2. Relationship with self:

. . . .

. . . .

3. Relationship with others:

. . . .

. . . .

CHAPTER 20

Emotional Robustness

What is emotional robustness?

Emotional robustness is your ability to navigate through, adapt and 'bounce back' from life's challenges, with patience (sabr), emotional strength, steadfastness and trust in Allah (swt) (tawakkul), without becoming overwhelmed or emotionally dysregulated yourself.

Emotional robustness not only shows strength and steadfastness in the face of adversity, but also doesn't avoid or dismiss the difficulties themselves or how you feel. Instead, robustness allows you to be a sturdy emotional 'container' to connect to, hold and contain, process and express your full emotions, for a healthy outlook and outcome on the situation.

Emotional robustness is important for you to be able to handle stress, overcome challenges and difficulties, recover swiftly from overcoming hardships, build confidence and support your problem-solving skills, which are all essential for your wellbeing.

The building blocks of emotional robustness

Boundaries	Gratitude	Patience	
Maintain perspective	Nurture connections	Positive actions	Emotional regulation
Self-growth	Self-compassion	Self-awareness	
Connection with Allah (swt)	Resilient mindset	Problem-solving skills	Learn from experiences

Building blocks of emotional robustness

You can build your emotional robustness through these building blocks. Interestingly, many of them are covered in the various chapters in this book for you to look through individually and work on each one.

In brief, these building blocks are:

- **Boundaries:** You set boundaries to protect your energy, time and capacity to prevent stress and overwhelm. (See Chapter 22: Boundaries.)

- **Gratitude (shukr):** You practise gratitude to focus on opportunities and foster a positive outlook on life. (See Chapter 6: Gratitude.)

- **Patience: (sabr):** You practise patience by accepting difficulties as life's tests and showing up with calmness and reflective, thoughtful responses rather than reactive and impulsive actions and behaviours.

- **Maintain perspective:** Through faith, you hold in mind this temporary world and focus on the Hereafter (Akhirah).

- **Nurture connections:** You cultivate your relationships and support circle. You nurture relationships which are positive, comforting and emotionally available to you. (See Chapter 24: Community and Support Circles.)

- **Positive actions:** You perform good deeds and acts of charity to foster your purpose in life. (See Chapter 12: Self-Values.)

- **Emotional regulation:** You recognize and manage your emotions in a healthy way, to support yourself to stay calm when you feel overwhelmed or emotionally dysregulated. (See Chapter 21: Emotional Regulation.)

- **Self-growth:** You seek knowledge and self-improvement. You pursue personal development and cultivate a growth mindset. (See Chapter 16: Self-Growth.)

- **Self-compassion:** You show kindness, love and compassion to yourself, especially during hardships. You stop and challenge any negative self-talk or criticism and replace it with positive self-talk, beliefs and affirmations. (See Chapter 14: Self-Compassion.)

- **Self-awareness:** You reflect on your feelings, triggers and responses to understand how you emotionally feel and react to challenging situations. You adopt a reflective or journaling practice to support deeper self-awareness. (See Chapter 17: Emotions for how to process emotions and Chapter 10: Self-Love for a daily wellbeing journal template.)

- **Connection with Allah (swt):** You establish regular prayer, supplication and remembrance of Allah (swt) to build a deeper connection with Him and to support your emotional regulation and stability. (See Chapter 5: Relationship with Allah (swt).)

- **Resilient mindset:** You cultivate a resilient, hopeful and optimistic outlook. You view challenges as opportunities for self-growth and personal development. You practise and develop a positive mindset and self-talk dialogue. (See Chapter 8: Self-Sabotage and Inner Critic.)

- **Problem-solving skills:** To stop feeling overwhelmed, you break down problems into smaller steps and solutions. You act systemically in your approach to problem solving. You ask your support circle for help, advice and support. You approach any challenge with a problem-solving attitude and belief in your ability to overcome any difficulties and setbacks.

- **Learn from experiences:** You view past experiences with hindsight and use your learning and lessons for self-growth, and carry this learning forward with you. You identify the strengths and solutions that you previously used to reapply them again in current situations and experiences. You acknowledge your legacy of overcoming challenges and your use of skills and experience to accomplish your goals and to surmount difficulties in the future.

Building emotional robustness takes time and consistent effort, but by practising these building blocks, you can help yourself develop a strong foundation inside and out for handling adversity and challenges. Each building block of emotional robustness helps reinforce a mindset and skillset that enables you to navigate life's challenges with greater adaptability, optimism and self-assurance.

Although emotional robustness doesn't eliminate the challenges, setbacks or problems themselves, emotional robustness does provide you with a solid foundation to navigate them effectively from a position of emotional stability and wellbeing.

REFLECTIONS

Can you identify which emotional robustness building blocks you feel and experience as some of your strengths?

. . . .

. . . .

. . . .

Which of the building blocks do you want to strengthen as part of your emotional robustness?

. . . .

. . . .

. . . .

How could you build these building blocks? What can you do to strengthen and grow them? What would you do? How might you do that? (See Chapter 16: Self-Growth to develop this into a growth plan.)

. . . .

. . . .

. . . .

How might you already be practising building some or all of these building blocks? What are you currently doing to strengthen them?

. . . .

. . . .

. . . .

Are there any actions, behaviours or habits that you are already practising but could be more intentional about? What would you do? How might you do that?

. . . .

. . . .

. . . .

What are your reflections from this chapter?

. . . .

. . . .

. . . .

Are there any self-growth goals you want to set for yourself, to support your development of emotional robustness?

. . . .

. . . .

. . . .

What emotional robustness actions or practices can you add to your self-care plan (see Chapter 4)?

. . . .

. . . .

. . . .

How can these practices and exercises further support your three relationship dimensions?

1. Relationship with Allah (swt):

. . . .

. . . .

2. Relationship with self:

. . . .

. . . .

3. Relationship with others:

. . . .

. . . .

CHAPTER 21

Emotional Regulation

What is emotional regulation?

Emotional regulation is the ability to manage and respond to emotional experiences in a healthy, constructive way.

It involves recognizing and acknowledging emotions as they arise, understanding their causes and purpose, and using strategies to manage them through practical techniques and spiritual practices. This supports you to feel emotionally regulated without letting emotions overwhelm you, your thoughts and behaviours.

Emotional regulation supports you to stay within your 'window of tolerance' (Siegel, 1999), which is your optimal zone of arousal. In this 'window', you feel regulated, balanced and in control. Emotional regulation is essential for your wellbeing as it informs your ability to maintain healthy relationships (with yourself and others), pursue personal growth and self-development, manage stressful or challenging situations, make informed decisions, behave and respond from an emotionally settled state, and express emotions authentically, responsively and with self-control.

Emotional dysregulation is the inability to manage, regulate and respond to emotional experiences; instead, it is an immediate emotional reaction to the trigger. Dysregulation pushes you outside of your 'window', either into hyper-arousal (heightened anxiety, overwhelm, extreme or impulsive reaction, anger, emotional outbursts or mood swings) or hypo-arousal (shutting down, feeling numb or disconnected, supressed emotions). These reactions can lead to behaviours, actions or decisions that are harmful, destructive or unproductive to the trigger, situation or relationship.

Practices for emotional regulation

Here are 20 practical techniques and spiritual practices for emotional regulation. Practising these techniques over time will increase your ability to stay emotionally settled and calm when feeling overwhelmed or under pressure and respond instead of reacting from impulse. Also the more you practice these, the easier and quicker you may find yourself being brought back into your emotionally settled state.

Grounding techniques	Breathing exercises	Mindfulness practices	Visualization techniques	Movement
Engaging the senses	Delay response	Cognitive reframing	Patience	Trust
Self-awareness	Gratitude	Self-compassion	Creative outlets	Safe environment
Mindful distractions	Boundaries	Daily routine	Problem-solving skills	Support

Emotional regulation practices

1. Grounding techniques

Grounding techniques help you to regain control and focus on the present.

- **5-4-3-2-1 technique:** Identify five things you can see, four things you can touch, three things you can hear, two things you can smell and one thing you can taste. This brings all your senses into present awareness and focuses on your immediate surroundings, physical sensations and present moment.

- **Physical contact:** Place your hands on your heart to reconnect with your body in the moment. Press your feet into the ground or your hands against the wall to anchor your body and feel stable in the moment.

- **Connect to nature:** Get outdoors into fresh air or nature to reconnect to the world around you.

- **Self-compassionate touch:** Give yourself a gentle hug to feel calm and connected to yourself.

- **Comfort object:** Hold a comforting object to bring you back into the moment and reconnect to feelings of calm, safety and relaxation.

2. Breathing exercises

Deep breathing helps calm the nervous system, slows down your heart rate and promotes relaxation. Count your breaths to keep focus on the breathing rate.

- **4-7-8 breathing:** Inhale for 4 seconds, hold for 7 seconds and exhale for 8 seconds. Repeat until feeling relaxed or returning to a relaxed state.

- **Box breathing:** Inhale for 4 seconds, hold for 4 seconds, exhale for 4 seconds and hold for 4 seconds. Repeat until feeling relaxed or returning to a relaxed state.

- **Diaphragmatic breathing (deep breathing):** Breathe deeply into the diaphragm rather than shallowly in the chest. Inhale deeply for 4 seconds through the nose, hold for 4 seconds and exhale slowly for 6 seconds through the mouth. Repeat as needed.

3. Mindfulness practices

Use mindfulness practices to bring you back into the present moment through focusing on your words, your body or your environment.

- **Remembrance of Allah (swt) (Dhikr):** Recite Allah's (swt) names or make supplications (dua) to bring about calmness, stay present in the moment and feel connected to Allah (swt).

- **Body scan meditation:** Focus your attention on your body. Mentally take a scan of your body from the top of your head down to your toes, noticing and releasing sensations or tensions in your body. This brings you back into your body and promotes relaxation and safety.

- **Mindful observation:** Choose an item in your immediate environment and bring your full focused attention to it. Examine the object closely. This anchors you back into the present moment.

4. Visualization techniques

Access imagery to feel stable and calm.

- **Calm place visualization:** Close your eyes and imagine a calm, peaceful place. Fill in the detail and focus on it. Picture the sights, sounds, smells. What can you see, hear, feel, smell and taste? Create a calm mental refuge for yourself to go to when you need to feel calm or relaxed.

- **Anchor visualization:** Imagine a solid tree with deep roots, or a huge mountain or an anchor at the bottom of the ocean, unmoving and steady. Imagine what it feels like to be that object. Feel your way into feeling solid, steady and anchored.

5. Movement

Engage in physical movement to release energy, reduce stress and bring your body into a calm state.

- **Gentle movement:** Praying, stretching, walking, tai-chi or any gentle movement helps release tension from the body and connects mindful activity with relaxation.

- **Movement breaks:** Take short movement breaks (stretches, walking) throughout the day, especially if sitting down or at a desk all day.

- **Regular exercise:** Engage in regular exercise that you enjoy to help release endorphins. Experiment and try out different physical activities to see which feel good for you.

- **Progressive muscle relaxation:** Starting from the bottom of your body and moving to the top, tense each muscle group and relax in turn. Move through your body to physically release tension and feel muscles relax.

- **Playfulness:** Play games, sports or activities that are fun, enjoyable and joyful, to release stress and tension and feel calm and safe.

6. Engaging the senses

Use soothing scents or sensory experiences to calm and relax you or ground you in the moment.

- **Warm compress:** Apply a warming compress, hot water bottle or heat pad to warm the muscles for relaxation.

- **Cold therapy:** Splash or spray cold water on to your face or hold a cool item, to reduce over-stimulation and hyper-arousal symptoms, and to anchor you back in the present.

- **Scents:** Use soothing scents and essential oils (e.g. lavender) to soothe and calm you. This could be a scented candle, incense, mist spray or fragranced body wash/lotion to help you unwind.

- **Sensory objects:** Use sensory objects, such as a weighted blanket, sensory toys or soft and comfortable clothing, to comfort you.

7. Delay response
Delay your response to any activating or triggering situation, stimuli or experience.

- **Pause before responding:** Take a moment before responding. Count to 20 (or any number needed) to move you from reaction to response. Do a breathing exercise to focus on your breathing rather than impulsive reaction.

- **Step away:** If you feel overwhelmed, step away from the situation. Go for a walk, get some fresh air, recite affirmations or make supplications (dua) for patience, to allow your emotions to settle and get back to a rational, calm responsive state.

8. Cognitive reframing
Reframe your thoughts to positive, affirming and constructive responses.

- **Question negative thoughts:** Identify negative thoughts as they arise. Challenge their validity. Is there evidence for this? Is it just a thought rather than fact? Is it an interpretation? Could there be an alternative perspective? (See Chapter 8 for more on negative self-talk and positive dialogue.)

- **Use positive self-talk:** Reframe negative thoughts into positive dialogue. Speak with a self-compassionate, supportive voice. What would be kind for you to hear right now? Remind yourself that feelings are temporary and that you are safe.

- **Practise positive affirmations:** Recite positive affirmations and statements about yourself – 'I am okay, I am safe', 'This is temporary', 'I can manage this', 'I can get through this' – to bring yourself into a calmer, relaxed state. (See Chapter 8 for a list of positive affirmations.)

- **Reality-checking:** Remind yourself of being in the present moment. Tell yourself what is happening right now, where you are, who you are with, what the situation is. This helps to ground you in the present reality.

9. Patience

Patience helps you to pause and reflect instead of reacting.

- **Practise patience (sabr):** Pause before reacting or replying immediately. Delay your response. Remind yourself of the blessings and guidance from Allah (swt) of the practice of patience, to help you remain calm and composed. Remind yourself of the possible negative consequences and damage caused by reacting and unthoughtful replies.

10. Trust

Place trust in Allah (swt) (tawakkul).

- **Affirm your trust in Allah (swt):** Intentionally speak to placing your trust in Allah (swt). Recite an affirmation of this intention – 'My trust is in Allah (swt)'. Putting your trust in Allah (swt) removes your potential reactions or heightened emotions, as you place the control and outcome with Allah (swt), reliant on His wisdom for the best outcome for you.

11. Self-awareness

Identify what you are feeling, to know how you are emotionally activated by a situation.

- **Identify emotions:** Name what you are feeling. Notice what you are doing with this feeling, wanting to avoid or dismiss it, have an outburst or shut down. Journal or write down how to manage your feelings and what you want to do with them. (See Chapter 17: Emotions for how to process emotions.)

- **Notice triggers:** Identify any patterns for the type of trigger, situations or experiences that leave you feeling emotionally overwhelmed or dys-regulated. Understanding what these patterns are will help you to prac-tise some of the practical techniques mentioned above, to help anchor you and bring you back to being emotionally regulated.

12. Gratitude

Gratitude focuses and reminds you of positive experiences and blessings in your life to help regulate feelings of overwhelm, sadness, frustration or hurt.

- **Identify positive experiences and successes:** Recall positive times in your life, especially where your strengths shone. Remember the challenges, obstacles and difficulties you have overcome. Remind yourself of your emotional robustness and positive mindset to deal with life's challenges. Remember this life is temporary, and you are striving for the Hereafter (Akhirah).

- **Keep a gratitude journal and habit:** List daily what you are grateful for. This could be in a journal, or you could recall three things as you wake up or go to sleep. This supports positive feelings of gratefulness, contentment and fulfilment, bringing an emotional calmness and stability. (See Chapter 6 for more on gratitude.)

13. Self-compassion

Treat yourself with kindness, love and care towards all your feelings without judgement to help soothe you.

- **Be kind:** Give yourself kindness and understanding, as you would to your loved ones. Don't criticize, blame or judge yourself for becoming emotionally upset or dysregulated. Recognize that feelings and emotional responses are part of human nature. It's okay not to be okay.

- **Practise forgiveness:** Forgive yourself if you have reacted, had an outburst or shut down. These have been your default ways of dealing with overwhelm or dysregulation. Don't shame yourself for how you have reacted. You are now learning and growing through these experiences.

- **Soothing self-talk:** Talk to yourself with compassion. Use positive self-talk and affirmations to reassure yourself that you are feeling safe and calm, or that however you are feeling is okay; to reduce any tension or inner conflict you are holding in your dialogue and associated beliefs.

- **Comfort activities:** Engage in comforting activities that soothe and calm you and which support you to feel safe. This could be any activity, hobby or interest that feels good to you (e.g. reading, comfort TV, playing a sport, walking, swimming) – anything that is comforting to you. (See Chapter 14 for more on self-compassion.)

14. Creative outlets

Engaging in creative activities helps to express and process emotions for regulation.

- **Arts and crafts:** Engage in creative arts and crafts (drawing, painting, crafting) to express your emotions, to help you identify what you are feeling and why. By releasing energy, you can support yourself towards calmness and relaxation.

- **Journaling:** Write down your feelings, to reflect on and process them. It helps reduce mental overwhelm or spiralling and bring perspective. This can help to identify triggers and patterns of response/reactions. (See Chapter 17 on processing emotions.)

15. Create a safe or calm environment

Create a space that soothes, relaxes and calms you.

- **Physical environment:** Be intentional about your spaces, especially your bedroom and living room (spaces for sleeping, resting and relaxing). Create a clutter-free, calming environment that doesn't over-stimulate or overwhelm you. It can include comforting objects and soothing sensory stimuli (e.g. soft furnishings and lighting, calming colours, soothing scents, relaxing sounds and comforting personal items).

16. Mindful distractions

Engage in mindful, absorbing activities to soothe you, take a mental break and bring you to a calm state.

- **Absorbing activities:** Engage in absorbing, light, uplifting hobbies or interests (e.g. baking, reading, gardening, drawing or doodling), to give your mind a rest from overwhelming feelings and to experience a calm, settled state.

17. Boundaries

Set limits to manage your energy, feelings and capacities to support you from feeling overwhelmed or dysregulated.

- **Establish boundaries:** Practise saying no to manage your energy and capacity levels and to prevent burnout. (See Chapter 22 for more on boundaries.)

- **Set limits:** Identify limits for activities, people or spaces which drain your energy.

- **Self-care:** Ensure time and space for self-care, which supports you to emotionally recover from overwhelm and dysregulation.

18. Daily routine

Create structures, habits and routines to prevent overwhelm and support emotional regulation.

- **Time management:** Use a planner to organize your day, identify your tasks and create a timeline for the day to help manage your time.

- **Daily routine:** Establish a consistent daily routine to create stability and predictability, which can set up habits to make the routine as effortless and effective as possible, and remove the need for additional decisions, which can lead to overwhelm and panic.

19. Problem-solving skills

Problem-solving skills support confidence and emotional robustness to deal with emotional dysregulation and ground you back into feeling regulated.

- **Identify small steps:** Break down solutions into small steps. Take each step one at a time without rushing or panic. This will support calmness and a sense of control over the situation.

- **Focus on what you can do:** For problems and solutions, focus on what is within your ability to do. Don't get caught up in what is outside of your reach. Make decisions and act where you can. Focus on what is productive and supports positive outcomes. This reduces stress and anxiety, as you feel an element of control.

20. Support

Access support via your support circle and/or professionals to find perspective, alternative outcomes and to feel contained, safe and calm. (See Chapter 24 for more on support circles.)

- **Share with a loved one:** Speak openly and honestly with a trusted, loved one. Sharing your experience and emotions helps to feel reassured, supported and calmer. Speaking it out loud helps to find perspective on the situation.

- **Professional help:** Speak with a therapist for professional support to learn emotional regulation tools and techniques, triggers for emotional dysregulation and coping skills for stress and overwhelm.

Practise these techniques to help you emotionally regulate. Find out what works for you to bring you back into a calm, soothed state. Incorporating these practices into your daily self-care and wellbeing plan supports emotional balance, robustness and appropriate responses to triggers.

Which of these emotional regulation techniques are you already using?

. . . .

. . . .

How effective are they? Could you practise them in any alternative way?

. . . .

. . . .

Which of these emotional regulation techniques would you like to practise? How might you do this?

. . . .

. . . .

Which techniques or practices would you like to incorporate into your daily routine? What would you do? How might you do that?

. . . .

. . . .

Use the Emotional Regulation Daily Checklist to help you incorporate these techniques and practices into a daily routine.

EMOTIONAL REGULATION DAILY CHECKLIST

> **Morning routine**
>
> **Set intention for the day**
>
> How do you want to show up emotionally today?
>
> . . . .
>
> . . . .
>
> Is there any situation that you may experience as emotionally dysregulating (e.g. a meeting, conversation or task)? How do you want to feel in that situation?
>
> . . . .
>
> **Gratitude practice:** Note 3 things you are grateful for:
>
>   1. . . . .
>
>   2. . . . .
>
>   3. . . . .
>
> **Positive affirmation:** How do you want to positively think about yourself today?
>
> . . . .
>
> . . . .
>
> **Dua:** What do you want to ask for, for today:. . . . .

> **Throughout the day**
>
> **Emotional check-in:** How are you feeling and why? What do you need to do to take care of your feelings?
>
> **Grounding techniques (if feeling overwhelmed):** 5-4-3-2-1 – notice 5 things you can see, 4 things you can touch, 3 things you can hear, 2 things you can smell, 1 thing you can taste.
>
> **Box breathing:** Inhale for 4 seconds, hold for 4 seconds, exhale for 4 seconds and hold for 4 seconds. Repeat until feeling relaxed or returning to a relaxed state.
>
> **Body scan meditation:** Focus your attention on your body. Mentally take a scan of your body from the top of your head down to your toes, noticing and releasing sensations or tensions in your body.
>
> **Calm place visualization:** Create a calm mental refuge for yourself to go to when you need to feel calm or relaxed.
>
> **Positive affirmations:** What positive affirmations can you recite to yourself to feel calmer?

cont.

Evening routine

Journaling: Reflect on your feelings and experiences from the day. Identify triggers and your responses.

. . . .

. . . .

Relaxation activities/creative outlets: What relaxing activity can you do this evening?

. . . .

. . . .

Prepare for tomorrow: Write down any thoughts, worries, tasks or goals for tomorrow:

. . . .

. . . .

Gratitude practice: Note 3 positive experiences or achievements from today:

1. . . . .

2. . . . .

3. . . . .

Dua: What do you want to ask for, at the end of your day:

. . . .

. . . .

Daily

Prayer:

Fajr ☐

Zuhr ☐

Asr ☐

Maghrib ☐

Isha ☐

Weekly

Weekly review prompt: At the end of the week, take time to reflect on emotional patterns and progress.

REFLECTIONS

What are your reflections from this chapter?

. . . .

. . . .

. . . .

Are there any self-growth goals you want to set for yourself, to support your development or practice of emotional regulation?

. . . .

. . . .

. . . .

Which emotional regulation practices can you add to your self-care plan (see Chapter 4)?

. . . .

. . . .

. . . .

How can these practices and exercises further support your three relationship dimensions?

1. Relationship with Allah (swt):

. . . .

. . . .

2. Relationship with self:

. . . .

. . . .

3. Relationship with others:

. . . .

. . . .

CHAPTER 22

Boundaries

Why are boundaries important?

Building healthy boundaries with yourself and in your relationships is an essential part of personal growth and wellbeing. Healthy boundaries will support you to nurture a healthy relationship with yourself, to be able to show up fully for yourself in your life and in your relationships, meet your needs and improve your wellbeing.

Boundaries for your wellbeing are the limits you set to protect your emotional, mental, physical, spiritual, financial, professional and social health. They are a message to yourself of the love and respect you have for yourself. Boundaries define how you relate to and interact with others and yourself, ensuring your needs, values, capacity and limits are respected. Setting boundaries in your life, with others and yourself, helps to create a balance between what you want and can give to others and what you need and want to keep for yourself, to be able to establish and maintain a sense of healthy wellbeing.

Boundaries, which call upon your personal power to help you maintain your sense of identity, autonomy and self-respect, are important to protect yourself from systems of oppression and structural inequalities. They empower you to prioritize your wellbeing without guilt, which is often how marginalized identities and communities can feel when enforcing boundaries, while holding on to and recognizing that setting boundaries is an essential act of radical self-care and wellbeing. This boosts your self-esteem and autonomy, by validating and honouring the truth and validity of your needs, feelings, values and decisions. Supporting your self-care and ensuring you don't over-extend or over-exert yourself nurtures healthy relationships with yourself and others, which fosters mutual respect and understanding.

Establishing and maintaining healthy boundaries can be a gradual process that involves self-awareness and self-compassion, as well as consistent practice, as you start to recognize your needs and limits and begin to introduce daily habits that support your boundaries. Remember that your boundaries will evolve and adjust over time, as they reflect what you need at different times in your life.

Signs of healthy boundaries

Key habits that illustrate healthy boundaries include:

- **Self-awareness:** You regularly check in with yourself to identify your needs and how you can meet them. You can recognize where your limits and boundaries are in respect to meeting your needs, knowing when you've crossed your own boundary or need to adjust your boundary to ensure you are meeting your needs to an optimal degree.

- **Self-respect:** You practise self-respect, including respecting and meeting your needs for optimal wellbeing, and feeling worthwhile and valued to have your needs met through healthy boundaries.

- **Communicate clearly:** You express your thoughts, feelings and needs clearly, transparently and honestly. There is no expectation or assumption that others can 'mind-read' what you need. You actively engage in conversations to state your boundaries to others, from an 'I' position, which does not blame and guilt-trip anyone, alongside being open to hearing other people's boundaries, which are mutually respected.

- **Consistency:** You consistently hold and respect your boundaries, reinforcing them when necessary. If boundaries are broken too often, this leads to a message that your boundaries, needs and wellbeing are unimportant, insignificant and not to be respected. Not reinforcing your boundaries undermines your self-respect, values and beliefs. This is not to say that your boundaries can't be flexible, but boundaries are not to be disrespected, ignored or dismissed by yourself or others.

- **Able to say no:** You can decline offers, favours or requests with politeness, without feeling guilty or anxious. See the 'How to say no' box at the end of the chapter.

- **Respect personal space:** You maintain and respect your own and others' physical boundaries and personal space.

- **Prioritize self-care appropriately:** You schedule regular time for activities that support your wellbeing, such as exercise, hobbies or relaxation.

- **Communicate limits:** You are self-aware of your limits and communicate them clearly. This might include saying no to a commitment for the following week, as you already know how emotionally and physically 'full' you are feeling and will not have the capacity for that engagement.

- **Engage in conflict constructively:** You approach conversations with a problem-solving mindset, seeking to understand the other's perspective and working collaboratively on the problem to solve it together. This may be scheduling uninterrupted time to have a conversation, hear one another's perspective and look to finding a solution which works to solve the problem and has an outcome that is positive for both.

- **Responsibility for yourself:** You hold responsibility for your own feelings and actions, and do not pass them on to or blame others. You do not take responsibility for other people's feelings or feel responsible for other people's happiness. You do not fall into the 'rescuer' position to take responsibility to 'fix' or 'rescue' others, especially when others do not take responsibility for themselves.

- **Nurture healthy relationships:** You surround yourself with people who are supportive and caring, where you nurture relationships, connections and communities, which are equal and beneficial to all and where you feel valued and respected. In relationships, boundaries are acknowledged and respected, fostering mutually healthy dynamics between you. Any discussions about boundaries are communicated with respect, understanding and compassion, with recognition that each other's boundaries are optimal for that person, even if they look different to one another.

- **Demonstrate flexibility in your boundaries:** You are flexible with your boundaries and can adjust them when you need to and out of choice, so your boundaries continue to be respectful to your needs, while navigating any relational changes or temporary changes to your schedule or commitments.

- **Manage emotional regulation and responses:** By practising reflective self-care and wellbeing practices, you are tuned in to your emotions and are reflective of your emotions in response to how others are behaving towards you. This supports you to know when you are being treated disrespectfully and/or when your boundaries are being crossed, so that you can take appropriate measures to re-establish your boundaries and return to an emotional place of safety, regulation and balance. This includes naming and communicating this breach in boundary and/or your feelings to others, from a place of emotional regulation and calm, and not from a place of reaction.

- **Centre personal beliefs and values:** You make decisions based on your core beliefs and values, which you communicate and assert for yourself, when being asked to do something or participate in an activity that doesn't align with you. You can stand up for yourself when you need to, without being aggressive or passive towards others when you communicate your boundaries to them.

- **Recognize the importance of mutual respect**: You recognize that your boundaries and other people's boundaries are to be respected equally and simultaneously. This supports mutually respectful relationships.

Types of boundaries

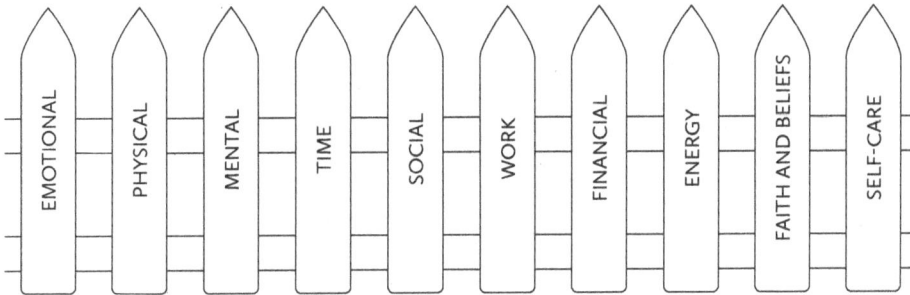

Ten types of boundaries

There are ten different types of boundaries to establish with yourself and others, which support your wellbeing. Here are the ten boundaries and practices of how you can establish them with yourself and others in your everyday life.

1. Emotional boundaries

Protect and respect your emotional energy and capacity by recognizing, understanding, managing and asserting how you feel and what emotional capacity you have for yourself and others.

Emotional boundaries with yourself: Recognizing, validating and expressing your emotions, as part of your experience, and not dismissing, invalidating or minimizing your emotions.

Emotional boundaries with others: Deciding and selecting which of your emotions you choose to share and who you choose to share them with. Choose people who feel trustworthy and safe or safe enough for you to share that aspect of your emotional life with. Decide how much emotional capacity and energy you have available and are willing to invest in your relationships. Choose not to carry or take on the responsibility for others' emotions, limiting the emotional capacity you hold for others. Say no to any activity that overwhelms you emotionally or stretches your emotional capacity, and limit your time and availability, to protect you from toxic, unsafe or harmful relationships and situations.

2. Physical boundaries
Protect and respect your physical space, energy and physical comfort, to feel safe and comfortable in your environment and relationships.

Physical boundaries with yourself: Listen to your physical limits and capacity. Take the time you need to rest and hold the balance between connecting and spending time with others and taking time out to spend in private and being with yourself.

Physical boundaries with others: Decide and set rules about your personal space, who can have physical contact with you and what your comfort level of physical contact looks like. Establish and communicate your own needs and capacity for personal space, touch and privacy. Identify your comfort levels for physical contact and establish your need for personal time, space and privacy.

3. Mental boundaries
Hold and honour your own thoughts, opinions, feelings, values and beliefs as your own 'truth' in their fullness and authenticity.

Mental boundaries with yourself: Hold your viewpoint in its full 'truth', without dismissing or minimizing your viewpoint or comparing your viewpoint with others and doubting your own viewpoint.

Mental boundaries with others: Protect your viewpoint from being dismissed, disrespected, minimized or rejected by others or from feeling under pressure to conform to others' thoughts, opinions, values, beliefs or expectations of you. If there is a challenge to your thoughts or viewpoint from others, respectfully respond to the challenge while asserting and holding your viewpoint without compromising it. This includes 'leaning back' or 'leaning out' of relationships or conversations where your viewpoint is being overpowered or where you experience feeling mentally drained by the other person.

4. Time boundaries

Respect your time and ensure your time is spent in alignment with your needs, values, ethics and goals, by establishing specific times for work, leisure, relationships and time alone.

Time boundaries with yourself: Identify and set aside time for yourself to meet your own individual needs (emotional, physical, mental, spiritual or psychological needs). This can include saying no to social events, allocating that time to yourself instead, or saying no to additional commitments (work or personal), which feel overwhelming or take you over your capacity and availability to fulfil that additional commitment.

Time boundaries with others: Set time limits and allocate time blocks for activities, including work, family, relationship and personal commitments. Choose to say yes to invitations that align with your priorities, values and time availability, and say no to those that don't. Identify your time boundaries in relationship with your other boundaries – for example, if you have limited emotional energy and availability, you can identify a limited time boundary for your availability that matches your energy or emotional capacity.

5. Social boundaries

Define the quality, nature and degree of your interactions and social connections with other people.

Social boundaries with others: Set time limits on how much time you spend with people, recognizing you will have different limits with different people, depending on how you experience your time with them. This is not just about the quantity of time spent with a person, but also recognizing what that quality of time feels like for you. Decide who you want to spend your time with, based on choosing to spend time with those who feel positive and supportive to you. Ask yourself: Does it feel nurturing or fun to spend time with this person? Does this time meet your emotional and relational needs? Is time with this person good for you?

6. Work boundaries

Respect and separate your working life from your personal life, to stop your working life leaking into your personal life and time. For example, set working hours within which you look at work emails or answer work phone calls, but do not do this outside of your working hours. Set boundaries around breaks or lunch time, to ensure you take your regular and necessary breaks throughout the day.

7. Financial boundaries

Identify, manage and budget how your money is spent and saved based upon your own priorities and within your means. For example, draw up a financial budget to control your money, identify where money gets spent and how much is saved towards identified future goals. This may mean identifying and allocating a specific amount for spending and saving each month and sticking to it.

8. Energy boundaries

Protect your energy by identifying how much energy you are choosing to invest in or spend on any activity, role or relationship. This includes recognizing and assessing your own energy levels, capacity and limits, paying attention to how much energy any task, activity or relationship will require at that time and knowing if you have enough energy or not to engage in that task or relationship. For example, set a time limit for what you can give to a task or relationship in that moment. It is important to honour your own energy levels and capacity, to engage without over-exerting yourself and giving yourself the time to rest and recover afterwards. Choose to prioritize time with those who energize and replenish your energy levels rather than with those who deplete your energy or place you in an environment that feels negative.

9. Faith, values and beliefs boundaries

Hold firm your personal values, faith and beliefs in their full 'truth' without compromising them. This includes making decisions and expressing your needs clearly, when they align and reflect your faith, core values and how you want to show up and relate to others in a space, and being able to do this from your beliefs and values position.

Faith, values and beliefs boundaries with yourself: Prioritize what is important to you, based on your faith, values and beliefs. For example, manage your day and time to prioritize your faith or belief practices, such as prayer and reading the Quran or Islamic books, or how you choose to balance the time you spend with family, friends and by yourself and manage your work–personal life balance.

Faith, values and beliefs boundaries with others: For example, this may be managing your working hours schedule to pray during the working day, requesting a prayer space or speaking up on what work social activities you are comfortable with and are able to participate in. A frequent example of this is a work culture of socializing at a pub or drinking alcohol. Holding to your beliefs boundary may look like you speaking to your line manager or work colleagues, explaining that this activity excludes you and asking if an inclusive and alternative option can be identified instead.

10. Self-care boundaries

Identify your individual self-care and personal needs, and protect your time to meet these needs.

Self-care boundaries with yourself: Honour and schedule time for rest and relaxation, engaging in hobbies and activities, and taking time for yourself and your self-care needs. Honour your self-care needs without guilt, as meeting your self-care needs is complimentary to meeting all your other needs and results in overall positive and healthy wellbeing.

Daily habits for healthy boundaries

Daily habits can support you, as foundations, to identify, establish and nurture healthy boundaries.

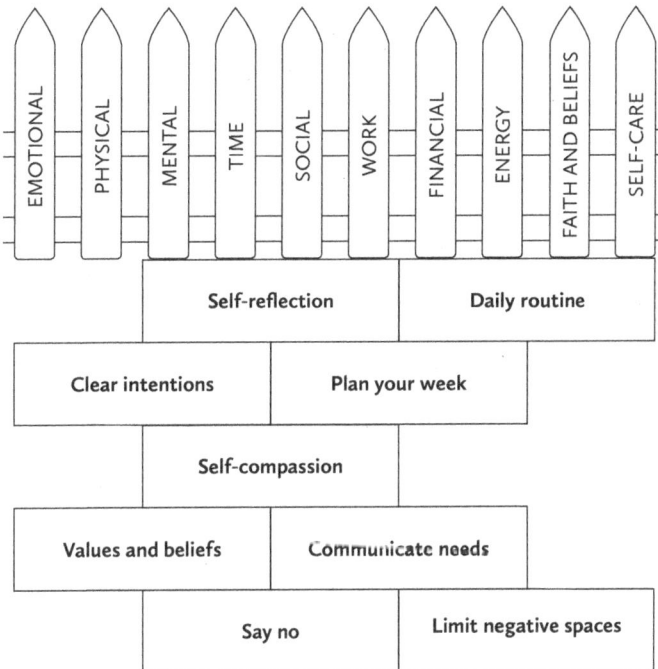

Daily habits for healthy boundaries

Here are the daily habits you can start to implement, to help build a daily practice of strengthening and maintaining your boundaries:

1. Practise self-reflection

Spend a few minutes each day reflecting on your thoughts, feelings and experiences from the day. Identify any time where you felt your boundaries were tested or overstepped and how you experienced that happening. How did you feel and respond? Were you able to name your boundary being overstepped? How might you have responded in a different way that would have supported your boundary? Could you have named that your boundary had been crossed and re-establish your boundary? Identify what you would say to the other person. This practice helps to identify if there is a pattern to what boundaries are crossed and how they are crossed, and find ways to respond in a manner that names, strengthens and re-establishes your boundary to be respected.

Spend a few minutes each day reflecting on how you are feeling. If you are feeling tired, exhausted or overwhelmed, where might you have overstepped your own boundaries and over-committed or not given yourself enough self-care time for rest and relaxation? Reflect on where and how you honour your own boundaries, where you don't prioritize your own boundaries and how you can reinforce your own boundaries.

2. Establish a daily routine

Identify which boundaries you can start to implement, or, if established, which boundaries you need to strengthen, in your daily life. Of the types of boundaries (see above), which boundaries do you need to implement or strengthen? Can you schedule your work boundaries? Can you identify how you spend your emotional energy throughout the day or week? Where and how can you put time boundaries in, to schedule time in your daily routine to meet your wellbeing needs (e.g. some much-needed 'me' time or time with family and friends)?

3. Set clear intentions

At the start of your day (this could be a practice before or after your fajr (morning prayers), identify and set your intentions for how you want to show up and approach your day. How do you want to feel? How do you want to be in your interactions? What do you want to make time for? What are you going to prioritize and block out time for today? What are you going to say no to? (Use the Emotional Regulation Daily Checklist in Chapter 21 to support this practice).

4. Plan your week

Set aside time at the start of each week to plan your week. This can be done in your diary or as a separate schedule (written or digitally). Write out your week, identifying the blocks of time spent on your commitments (work, family or other responsibilities). Having scheduled your commitments, next block out time for your choice of activities (hobbies, time with friends, time out, etc.). Decide if anything in your schedule doesn't work for you that week (e.g. if you don't have the emotional capacity or physical energy) and if you need to reschedule anything or say no to something. Identify if you need to move or establish any boundaries in relation to your schedule or commitments.

5. Practise self-compassion

Engage in regular self-compassion exercises, such as saying or writing out positive affirmations to yourself and speaking to yourself with kindness. This sends a regular message to yourself that you are valued, loved and cared for, by you. It reminds you that it's okay to honour and meet your needs, and to be able to put in boundaries which support your needs, wellbeing and overall health. (See Chapter 14: Self-Compassion to support this practice.)

6. Reflect on your values and beliefs

Identify your values and beliefs, and notice if they show up in your boundaries. Does your love and self-compassion reflect the boundaries you hold? Do your boundaries allow time to meet your needs? This practice can be built into your daily journaling and brought into your weekly planning, to ensure that your boundaries reflect and align with your values and beliefs and are implemented into your daily and weekly schedule. If you find that they don't align, adjust your schedule and boundaries to being them into alignment. For example, this could be spending more or less time with people or on your own, to optimize how best this time meets your needs. (See Chapter 12: Self-Values to support this practice.)

7. Communicate your needs:

Practice sharing your feelings and needs with others. This helps build communication, trust and safety in your relationships, without expectations or assumptions that others will know what you need from them. This will also support them to share with you what their needs are in your relationship. To build this into a habit, you may want to schedule a regular time (in your weekly schedule) for a check-in with your partner or family members, to share feelings and needs and what you need from each other in the coming week. For example, if you have a particularly busy week at work or additional family commitments that week, what do you need from your partner or family member to support you to navigate that week and for you to show up in the best way you can.

8. Learn to say no

It can feel challenging to say no, especially if you've been taught not to say no to your parents or elders. You've learnt how not to put boundaries in for yourself, and saying no can lead you to feeling guilty. This is because of the meaning attached to saying no. 'No' comes to mean rejection, rudeness and disrespect, whereas saying no, when a boundary is put in, is to define your limits and capacity. It is to communicate what you can and can't do, what capacity you have and what you are able to offer and do. Practise saying no from a new position and meaning of identifying your limit, capacity and availability. For example, you can offer an alternative day or time to meet with friends, when it suits you better, or say you don't have capacity or availability to say yes. This helps to manage better communication, without a boundary feeling as if you are being rude or disrespectful to the others. Use the 'How to say no' guide below to help you structure saying no.

9. Limit time in negative environments

Nurture an environment (in-person and online) that feels supportive and nurturing to you. Limit, unfollow or remove any online and social media platforms or accounts that don't align with your values and beliefs, and which don't support your wellbeing and lifestyle. Recognize any spaces or environments which leave you feeling not good about yourself or drained. These are not positive or fulfilling your needs. Set time boundaries for how long you spend online. Take digital detox days, where you spend 24 hours offline, or put in an offline boundary, where you designate certain hours in the day to not being online (e.g. for one hour before sleep). This supports your energy levels and helps you to connect and reconnect with people and those in person around you.

HOW TO SAY NO

Saying 'no' can feel uncomfortable. Here are ways to structure your 'no', with assertiveness and clarity of your boundaries.

- **Show gratitude first:**
  - Thank you for thinking of me.
  - I appreciate you thinking of me.
  - I really appreciate your thought/consideration.

- **Be positive towards what is being offered:**
  - It sounds like fun.
  - It sounds interesting.
  - It looks like something challenging and engaging to do.

- **Identify your current capacity:**
  - I am currently at full capacity.
  - I have a full work schedule at this time.
  - I am currently managing my full commitments.
  - I am focused on my studies/current role right now.

- **State your 'no', if unable to take up the offer:**
  - I'm unable to take on any new/additional commitments currently.
  - I really wish I could take this on and say yes but I'm at maximum capacity.
  - I'd love to take this on, but I know I don't have the time to give this the attention it needs.
  - I'll have to pass on this, unfortunately.

- **Offer a postponement, if applicable:**
  - Can I get back to you on this?
  - I will need to check my diary moving forward; let me get back to you shortly.
  - I can't give an answer straight away, but can we come back to this next week?

- **Offer an alternative, if suitable:**
  - I don't have the availability to do that, but I can do (alternative role/task) instead.

- **Keep the door open for future offers:**
  - Please do keep me in mind for any future opportunities.
  - Please do let me know of the next time you are thinking of doing this (social event/activity).
  - I'd love to join you next time; please let me know.

This approach offers a transparency of your capacity and limits, with you being able to put in a boundary and say 'no' respectfully, to maintain a positive communication with others and limit any conflicts or feelings of confrontation. You can say 'no' with honesty and self-respect, while valuing your own boundaries, values and beliefs.

TIPS FOR SETTING BOUNDARIES

- Be clear and specific when communicating your boundaries.
- Use 'I' statements when stating your needs, choices and decisions.
- Practise saying a soft 'no' by declining politely and offering an alternative if you want to and can.
- Maintain your boundaries consistently so that you are respecting your own needs.
- Express appreciation or gratitude for what is being asked or offered to you before responding with your soft 'no', as your no does not take away from the goodness or blessings in what is being asked of you.
- If saying 'yes' to an offer, invitation or request, set a time limit on how much time you can give.
- If unsure of your answer in the moment, put a hold or pause in place, by saying that you'll get back them by a certain time with an answer.
- Be honest about your capacity and availability. It's best to say a soft 'no' instead of a half-hearted 'yes', if you then struggle to fulfil the commitment and need to back out of your 'yes'.
- Show yourself self-compassion, recognizing that establishing and honouring your boundaries is good for your wellbeing and health.
- Remind yourself that you are valued and loved by sharing or saying some positive self-love affirmations to yourself.

REFLECTIONS

Which types of boundaries are you already practising and establishing? How are you able to establish them?

. . . .

. . . .

. . . .

How effective are they? Do they need any additional support or reinforcement?

. . . .

. . . .

. . . .

Which types of boundaries are new to you and/or do you recognize you need to set and establish? How might you do this? What steps will you take to practise these boundaries?

. . . .

. . . .

. . . .

Which boundary techniques or practices would you like to incorporate into your daily routine? What would you do? How might you do that?

. . . .

. . . .

. . . .

What are your reflections from this chapter?

. . . .

. . . .

. . . .

Are there any self-growth goals you want to set for yourself, to support your development of boundaries?

. . . .

. . . .

. . . .

Which boundary practices can you add to your self-care plan (see Chapter 4)?

. . . .

. . . .

. . . .

How can these practices and exercises further support your three relationship dimensions?

1. Relationship with Allah (swt):

. . . .

. . . .

2. Relationship with self:

. . . .

. . . .

3. Relationship with others:

. . . .

. . . .

Relationship with Others

'The believers, men and women, are Auliya' (helpers, supporters, friends, protectors) of one another...Allah will have His Mercy on them.' (9:71)

CHAPTER 23

Relationship with Others

We are hardwired for relationships and connections with others. Building relationships with others is essential to balanced and optimal wellbeing. By building strong and healthy relationships, you are nurturing your emotional robustness, sense of belonging and community, feeling of fulfilment, emotional support, personal goals and growth, shared experiences and healing through relationships, which all contribute towards your wellbeing. As with your self-relationship, you need to intentionally build and nurture good relationships with others. It is an ongoing process, as your relationships unfold and evolve over time. But by intentionally investing in these relationships (alongside your relationship with Allah (swt) and with yourself), you are looking after yourself for optimal wellbeing.

Belonging

Deeper to physically and emotionally being in relationship with others, a feeling of belonging is essential for wellbeing. Belonging is the deeply felt sense and experience of feeling accepted, valued and connected to those in your relationships, groups, family and community. It is a feeling of 'being at home' in the presence of the other person. It is feeling assured that who you are, in your fullness and authenticity, is valued and accepted, without judgement or fear. You can be your authentic, genuine self, without needing to change yourself. It fulfils the need to be seen, heard and met by others. To be embraced fully for who you are. Belonging offers and supports the comfort and safety needed for a healthy emotional bond, bringing peace to those in that relationship.

Belonging is cultivated through the experience of understanding, mutual trust and respect, and shared spaces of emotional intimacy and vulnerability. It is the ability to share feelings, thoughts, values, beliefs and experiences without being judged, criticized or negatively received by others. This supports a level of mutual respect to honour one another's perspectives and celebrate each person's uniqueness.

Belonging supports healthy relationships by fostering trust, vulnerability, honesty and respect, while also supporting your own emotional and mental robustness. Feeling a sense of belonging in groups and relationships supports you to feel more positive about yourself, as it leads to feeling less isolated and lonely, and builds your self-confidence, self-esteem, motivation and robustness.

Belonging is the opposite of 'fitting in'. Fitting in is needing to (or thinking you need to) change, mould or adapt yourself to meet other people's expectations of you to be accepted by them. Belonging doesn't require you to change who you are; it invites you to show up and be who you truly are.

Belonging and showing up authentically can be challenging for marginalized and minoritized identities, where you may feel pressure to 'fit in', in order to be accepted, alongside experiencing a lack of understanding, empathy and compassion for parts of your identity or lived experience. Fitting in may lead to 'dimming down', keeping away or silencing parts of you from conversations and relationships, if it feels that parts of you won't be accepted by others and stops you from feeling accepted. Although there is possible pressure to 'fit in', it has negative impacts on your wellbeing, as it knocks your self-esteem and self-confidence, and colludes with you self-abandoning yourself, moving you away from self-acceptance, self-love, self-compassion and your core values and beliefs. It stops you from having a healthy, positive self-relationship.

Belonging starts from within, from cultivating self-acceptance, confidence and authenticity, and showing up in relationships in your full, genuine identity and experience. It supports others in your relationships to mirror and cultivate true belonging within themselves and ultimately within the relationships between you, for shared acceptance, compassion and belonging.

Practices to develop a sense of belonging

Practices to develop a sense of belonging in your relationships include:

- **Affection:** Physical contact and intimacy, such as hugging, holding hands or any safe and comfortable physical touch or contact that respects physical boundaries, builds the intimacy between you and others, and promotes the deepening of bonding between you.

- **Communication:** Demonstrate clear communication by openly sharing your feelings and thoughts with others. Have regular check-ins with others to connect and attune to one another's experiences, feelings and thoughts, so that you can support mutual understanding and avoid misunderstandings or assumptions made.

- **Emotional intimacy:** Sharing vulnerabilities, feelings, thoughts, fears or dreams with others fosters an emotional intimacy between you, where understanding and being seen, heard, accepted and connected are developed to bring you closer to one another.

- **Independence:** While the relationship and experience of belonging nurture the connection between you and others, the relationship also accommodates the space you each need to independently and individually pursue your own self-growth, life and professional goals. You offer support to others; you cheer them on as they pursue their goals, while you also strive to meet your own.

- **Commitment:** Belonging is nurtured when you demonstrate and express commitment to relationships, through words, actions, gestures, celebrations or anniversaries. It could be as simple as words of affection, a small gift, a card or letter, through to planning an event together, celebrating an anniversary or planning for a future event, goal or experience.

- **Boundaries:** Establishing, maintaining and respecting boundaries – yours and others' – is essential to support feeling safe or safe enough in relationships. This helps you to have control over your experiences in any relationship, as well as having choice over what you share with others, what they know about you and how quickly the relationship develops, to build a healthy and safe/safe enough relationship at the appropriate pace for you.

- **Growth:** Supporting one another's growth recognizes and respects that each person will grow and evolve through life, both independently and through the relationship itself. It allows for individual growth while supporting the growth that occurs because each person is nurtured by the relationship itself.

- **Shared experiences:** Create memories and bonding experiences together by engaging in shared experiences. This could be a day out, a holiday, or everyday activities such as cooking a meal together, watching a film or TV show, or any shared interest activity that is meaningful to both of you.

- **Nurturing:** Show your care for others, through active listening, patience, holding space for them, respecting their time, offering encouragement, support and help when they need it, and being thoughtful towards them. You are showing that they matter to you and that you are present for them and care about their wellbeing too.

- **Forgiveness:** Offering forgiveness to one another, especially after conflicts or ruptures, builds the sense of belonging between you, as forgiveness brings hope, repair and safety to the relationship. Your willingness to resolve conflicts and repair any fractures in the relationship, to turn towards the other person, instead of avoiding or ignoring the conflict, communicates your respect and value for the relationship and your intentions to repair and fix the relationship itself.

- **Reassurance:** Share positive affirmations and reassurances to others about the relationship, to demonstrate your appreciation, happiness, or satisfaction with the relationship, such as 'I appreciate our friendship', 'I am so pleased we met', 'I'm so glad we're together' or 'I enjoy spending time with you'. This could be said verbally or written in a card, letter or text message.

- **Conflict resolution:** Looking at conflict resolutions and repairs as opportunities for growth, learning and insight about yourself, the relationship and each other becomes a growing space for the relationship to thrive and deepen the stability, safety and robustness of the relationship itself. Overcoming challenges to the relationship deepens your bond and unites you with others as being on the 'same page'.

- **Reliability:** Be reliable, consistent and dependable in your words and actions. Do, say and show up as you have communicated you would. Become someone who is not just seen but is experienced as being reliable. When you can be relied upon and can rely on others, this nurtures trust between you and others.

- **Vulnerability:** Practise being emotionally vulnerable with safe and trusted people. Share your feelings and thoughts to experience them being heard and met with empathy and non-judgement. Practise offering empathy and compassion in return when others are vulnerable with you. This builds the trust in your relationships.

- **Appreciation:** Show your appreciation for others to them. This could be a verbal appreciation of thanks, a thank-you card or a gift. Any gesture of appreciation demonstrates how much you value, respect and care for them, what they bring to the relationship and what they offer you through your relationship together. This reinforces the positive mutual connection between you.

- **Support:** Offer support to others by showing that you are present for them and that they can lean on you for help. Ask what they need help, advice or support with. If you know they are going through a difficult time, offer practical as well as emotional support through dropping off food, babysitting, helping them with any task or errand they need to do or offering to take something off their plate and fulfilling a task or job on their behalf.

- **Validation:** Validate each other's feelings, thoughts and experiences, even if you don't agree. By validating your own and other people's feelings, thoughts and experiences, you are respecting and honouring everyone's 'truth' for what it is for each of you. This honours your unique, individual lived experience, without it being compared to others or dismissed or invalidated as being 'less than' or not as important as others. This fosters mutual respect and honour for one another, and encourages you to feel safe or safe enough and that you belong in the relationship.

- **Acceptance:** Practise accepting fully what others share with you and notice if they can do the same for you. Accept without judgement. Accept that you and others are not perfect, so you will demonstrate and show up with flaws, mistakes and imperfections, sometimes getting things wrong, misunderstanding each other or, if having a 'bad' day, not having as much empathy, patience or support to offer one another. It is accepting yourself and others not just on your 'best' days but on every day and especially on a 'bad' day.

- **Autonomy:** Respecting yours and others' individuality and autonomy, both inside and outside of the relationship, communicates and reflects the respect and value shared between you.

- **Meaningful:** Identify what your shared values, goals or interests are and nurture time to be spent on these together. This could be embodying a shared value together such as engaging in charity work or volunteering together, supporting each other's goals or taking part in meaningful activities or interests together, such as walking, cycling, going to the gym, travelling or spending quality time with family/friends.

There are many ways to build healthy relationships. The following chapters in this section will explore four traits of healthy relationships in further detail, these traits being community and support circles, relationship blueprints, emotional intimacy and availability, and emotional safety, so that you can cultivate strong and healthy relationships with others for yourself.

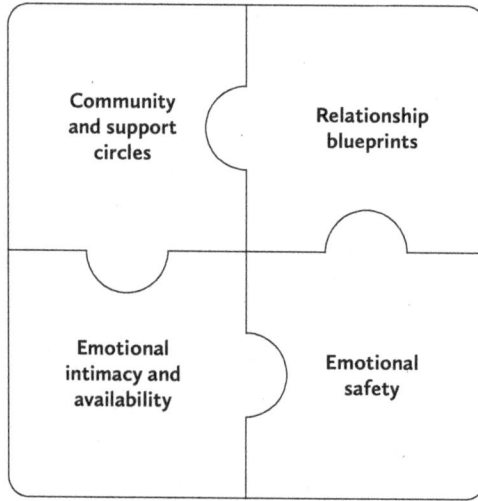

Four traits of healthy relationships

REFLECTIONS

What is your experience of belonging in relationships?

. . . .

. . . .

. . . .

How do you know, feel or experience a sense of belonging?

. . . .

. . . .

. . . .

Which of the belonging practices do you already employ?

. . . .

. . . .

. . . .

Are there any actions, behaviours or habits that you are already practising but could be more intentional about? What would you do? How might you do that?

. . . .

. . . .

. . . .

How do you want to nurture a sense of belonging in your relationships?

. . . .

. . . .

. . . .

What belonging practices might you want to start to cultivate in your relationships?

. . . .

. . . .

. . . .

Are there any self-growth goals you want to set for yourself, to support your development of belonging in relationships?

. . . .

. . . .

. . . .

What belonging actions or practices can you add to your self-care plan (see Chapter 4)?

. . . .

. . . .

. . . .

What are your reflections from this chapter?

. . . .

. . . .

. . . .

How can these practices and exercises further support your three relationship dimensions?

1. Relationship with Allah (swt):

. . . .

. . . .

2. Relationship with self:

. . . .

. . . .

3. Relationship with others:

. . . .

. . . .

CHAPTER 24

Community and Support Circles

Connection to support your wellbeing

Having community and support circles around you offers the opportunity for you to be emotionally and socially connected to others. This could range from your closest, dearest friends and family members to casual acquaintances.

Being connected to others, through community and support circles, offers support to your wellbeing in several ways:

- **Emotional bonding:** Through empathy, trust, kindness, compassion and forgiveness, you feel connected to others, understood in your feelings, valued and emotionally engaged, and you experience a space for open communication, which strengthens your emotional health and connections to others.

- **Communication:** Through open, honest dialogue, active listening and sharing experiences, feelings and thoughts, you experience genuine, meaningful connections, feeling understood, belonging and connected.

- **Support:** Giving and receiving emotional support, being present for others while they are also present for you, builds feelings of mutual emotional connection, care, belonging and support, reduces feelings of isolation and loneliness, and reconnects you to your immediate community and the wider Ummah.

- **Family:** A foundation of strong family bonds and healthy relationships provides emotional support, protection, nurture and sense of collective identity for healthy wellbeing.

- **Belonging:** Shared interests and faith or cultural identity, and connecting to a community through a shared identity foster a sense of authenticity, belonging and being seen and understood. This comes with an ease of integrating into a group as there are commonalities and mutual understanding.

- **Self-care:** Through encouragement and motivation for your growth or goals, relationships support your self-care practices and needs being met.

- **Collective growth:** Joint activities, mutual growth and development goals, and shared enthusiasm and positivity support collective growth for your community, increase your shared sense of achievement and endurance, and support shared success, healing and growth.

- **Balance:** Through connection and community, your needs for emotional and social connection are met, while balancing them with healthy boundaries and time for yourself, to optimally support your wellbeing through moderation of time alone and time with others.

Your support circles

Having broader community groups to feel a part of and your own unique support circle to belong in are both essential for your wellbeing.

A support circle is specifically your network of known people (family, friends, colleagues and community members), where you offer each other emotional, social and/or spiritual support through assistance, encouragement, advice, practical help, shared experiences and reflection. This fosters emotional robustness, motivation, perspective, belonging and self-growth, and reduces feelings of isolation and loneliness, when navigating life and its challenges. Essential to support circles are the components of trust, open communication, reciprocity and shared or common beliefs and values.

Identifying your support circle can help you to visualize and recognize your current relationships of support, any possible gaps in your support needs and how to strengthen your support circle.

Using the following support circle template, fill in the circles with the names of those who belong in each level of support.

The levels of support are:

- **inner circle:** closest relationships (partner, children, family, best friends)
- **middle circle:** good friends, trusted peers and colleagues, extended family members

- **outer circle:** casual friends and acquaintances, members of wider community.

Next to each name, note what type of support they offer you (e.g. emotional, social or spiritual support) and in what types of formats or spaces (e.g. nurturing space, compassionate space, advice, solutions, practical help, space to unwind and relax, encouragement, good listener, engaging in shared hobbies or interests).

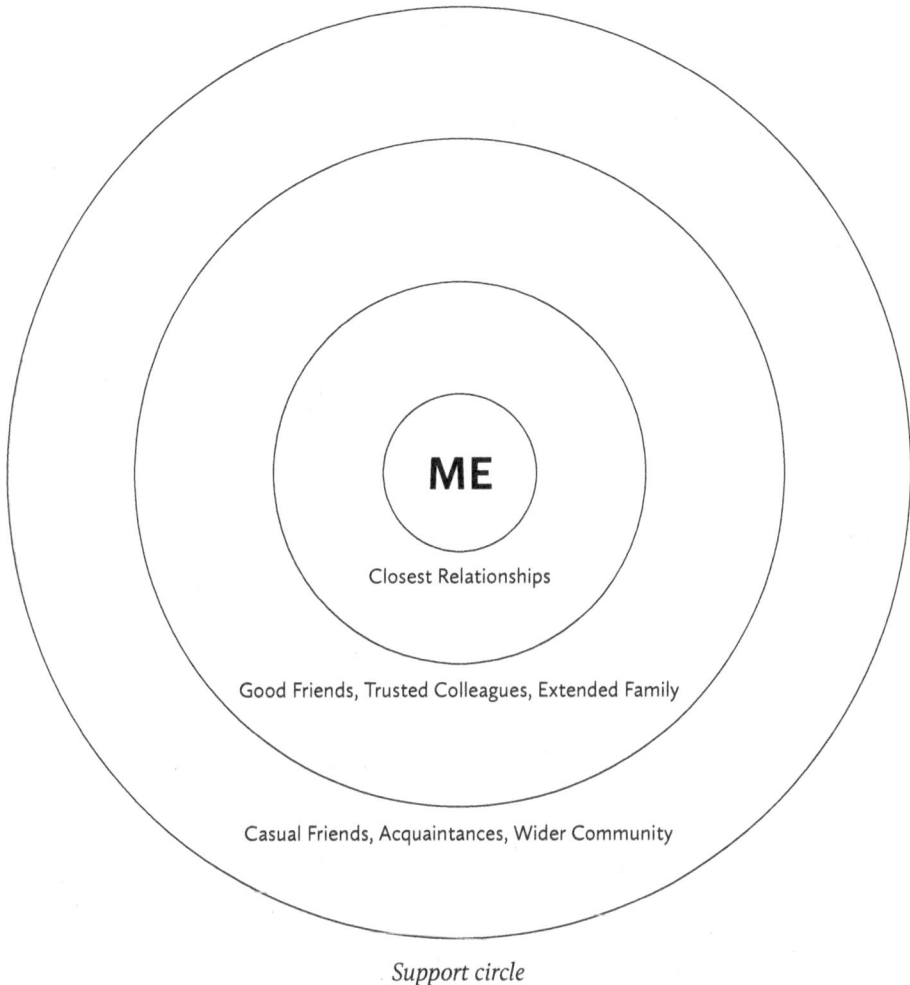

ME

Closest Relationships

Good Friends, Trusted Colleagues, Extended Family

Casual Friends, Acquaintances, Wider Community

Support circle

Having filled in your support circle, take some time to reflect on your unique support circle.

Does anything stand out or come to mind straight away, as you look and reflect on your support circle?

. . . .

. . . .

How does seeing your support circle feel to you?

. . . .

. . . .

Do you feel supported adequately or appropriately by those you've put in your support circle?

. . . .

. . . .

Is there anyone in your support circle you wish to build upon or strengthen your relationship with?

. . . .

. . . .

Are there any gaps of support in your support circle? Are there any areas in your life that could use more support (e.g. for your professional challenges, personal growth, spiritual/emotional/mental/physical health)?

. . . .

. . . .

To intentionally build or strengthen your support circle, what do you hope to achieve with your enhanced support circle? What needs are you looking to meet (e.g. for your emotional support, practical help, advice on a particular goal or task)? Be as specific as possible.

. . . .

. . . .

Is there anyone in your outer or middle circles who is positive, trustworthy and skilled, who could support you more?

. . . .

. . . .

In effective support circles, there are different support circle roles that people play and that you need in your support circle to meet your various needs.

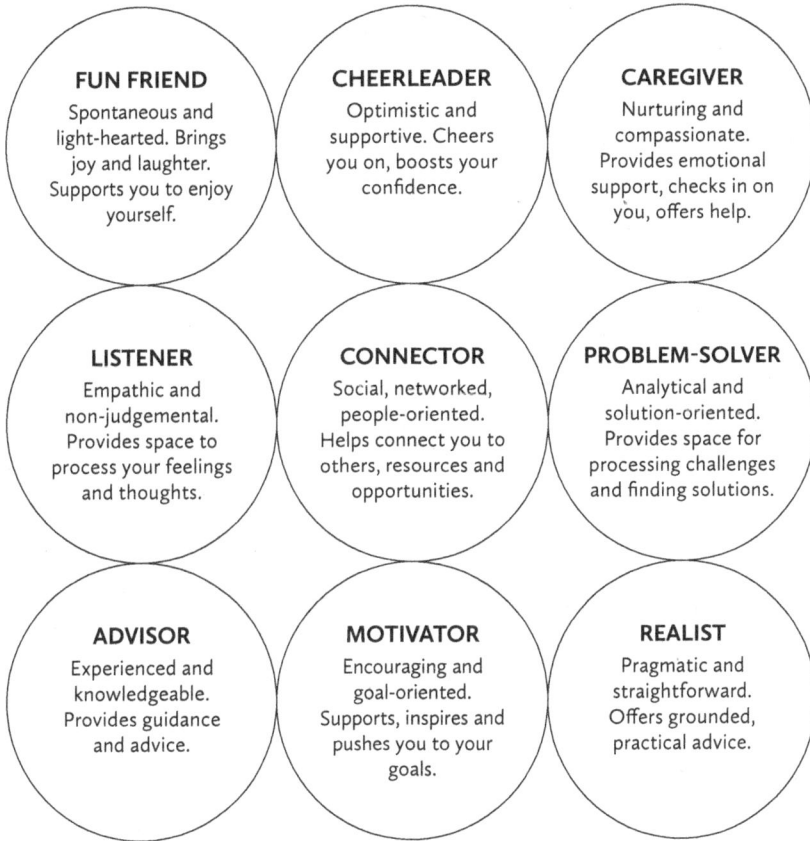

FUN FRIEND
Spontaneous and light-hearted. Brings joy and laughter. Supports you to enjoy yourself.

CHEERLEADER
Optimistic and supportive. Cheers you on, boosts your confidence.

CAREGIVER
Nurturing and compassionate. Provides emotional support, checks in on you, offers help.

LISTENER
Empathic and non-judgemental. Provides space to process your feelings and thoughts.

CONNECTOR
Social, networked, people-oriented. Helps connect you to others, resources and opportunities.

PROBLEM-SOLVER
Analytical and solution-oriented. Provides space for processing challenges and finding solutions.

ADVISOR
Experienced and knowledgeable. Provides guidance and advice.

MOTIVATOR
Encouraging and goal-oriented. Supports, inspires and pushes you to your goals.

REALIST
Pragmatic and straightforward. Offers grounded, practical advice.

Support circle roles

Filling gaps in your support circle

To identify if there any unfilled roles in your support circle, fill out the following table. Write next to each role: the people who fill that role in your current support circle, their characteristics (e.g. empathic, reliable, honest, solution-focused) and how they support you in their role (e.g. listen to you, identify solutions, offer advice, motivate you).

Support circle roles table

Roles	Names	Characteristics	Ways they support you
Fun friend			
Cheerleader			
Caregiver			
Listener			
Connector			
Problem-solver			
Advisor			
Motivator			
Realist			

Looking at the support circle roles table, are there any roles missing or going unfilled in your support circle? Who might that be (e.g. a mentor, coach, therapist, friends via shared interests, peers via shared profession)? What role do they play? What do you need from them?

. . . .

. . . .

. . . .

Identifying any gaps helps you to intentionally build and strengthen your support circle.

Recognizing any unfilled roles, how might you build those types of relationships? Do you need to expand your network? Who do you need to reach out to? Are there new acquaintances, groups or communities to tap into and build upon? Are there current networks, communities or groups that are being under-utilized (e.g. being part of an online group or community, joining in online activities, engaging in local networking and community groups and activities)?

. . . .

. . . .

. . . .

By understanding and recognizing the different types of people, roles and support you need, enhancing your support circle of people with the right characteristics and investing in healthy relationships is a rewarding process. You can be intentional in choosing which people (in their role) will be the best type of support for you and in which situation or space. You can choose who you need support from, what type of support and in which situation, area or space in your life. This ensures an optimal balance of support for your wellbeing, to navigate life's challenges, celebrate each other's wins and share the journey together.

Regularly revisit your support circle, to review and update, and possibly identify new or emerging gaps and roles to be filled, to maintain a healthy network and support circle for yourself.

REFLECTIONS

How are you currently building and strengthening your support circle? What do you do?

. . . .

. . . .

. . . .

How effective are your support circles? Do they need any additional support or reinforcement?

. . . .

. . . .

. . . .

Are there any particular roles that you need to build or strengthen at this time in your life?

. . . .

. . . .

. . . .

What are your reflections from this chapter?

. . . .

. . . .

. . . .

Are there any self-growth goals you want to set for yourself, to support your development of support circles?

. . . .

. . . .

. . . .

How can your support circle be added to your self-care plan (see Chapter 4)?

. . . .

. . . .

. . . .

How can these practices and exercises further support your three relationship dimensions?

1. Relationship with Allah (swt):

. . . .

. . . .

2. Relationship with self:

. . . .

. . . .

3. Relationship with others:

. . . .

. . . .

CHAPTER 25

Relationship Blueprints and Attachment Patterns

Attachment and emotional bonds

As we seek relationships and connections with others, our early experience of attachment and emotional bonds shapes and influences the foundation of our relationships throughout life. This early experience of attachment forms our attachment pattern. The attachment pattern is a repeated experience and expectation of the quality of emotional intimacy (trust, openness and vulnerability) and preoccupation (focus) in the relationship.

This attachment style forms our relationship blueprint, a framework of how to attach and bond in relationships, the degree of intimacy, stability and reassurance we seek in relationships, and how we respond to conflicts and ruptures and express our needs. It is this relationship blueprint that we find ourselves repeating unconsciously into our adult relationships of how we relate to others, through our actions, beliefs and expectations about relationships. Our relationship blueprint becomes a familiar way of relating to others, and as it is used as the blueprint for how to relate, it's why we experience the 'same' relationship dynamics but with different people. It's the same pattern but with different people on the receiving end of it.

Attachment styles

The four main types of attachment styles are secure, anxious, avoidant and disorganized, as shown in the following diagram (Levine and Heller, 2010).

SECURE	ANXIOUS
balance of closeness and independence	seeks closeness but fears abandonment or rejection
balanced sense of self-worth	
comfortable to express feelings, needs and boundaries	anxious about stability and security of relationship
seeks and offers support	expects relationships to feel uncertain
handles rejection without feeling devastated or overly anxious	may feel need to earn love and affection
	seeks reassurance from the other person
expects relationships to be safe	sensitive to perceived changes in relationship
believes conflicts and ruptures can be resolved	cycle of over-demanding then pushing away others, confirming belief they will be abandoned

ATTACHMENT STYLES

AVOIDANT	DISORGANIZED
values independence, self-reliance and autonomy	longs for closeness but equally afraid of it
avoids emotional intimacy	fears being abandoned
needs space and time for themselves	alternates between clinging to and pushing away others
sharing feelings, anxieties or difficulties feels too vulnerable or threatening	lacks trust in self and others
responds to conflicts by avoiding, distancing or shutting down	believes relationships can be comforting but also unreliable or dangerous
expects relationships to feel too close	cycle of swinging between getting too close and withdrawing, confirming belief that relationships are unstable and volatile
cycle of distancing when others get close, relationship becomes strained, confirming belief that closeness is threatening or unsafe	

Four attachment styles

The attachment styles are defined by two dimensions (see the following figure) – a dimension of intimacy and a dimension of preoccupation – and where you land on each dimension indicates your attachment style (Levine and Heller, 2010).

The dimension of intimacy is the degree of emotional intimacy that you find optimal and most comfortable. This can range from maximum intimacy (high comfort with emotional closeness) to minimum intimacy (low comfort with emotional closeness or avoidance of intimacy).

The dimension of preoccupation is the degree to which you think about and are preoccupied about your relationship, and the degree of anxiety about the other person's love and affection for you. This can range from maximum preoccupation (high relationship anxiety and spending much of your time thinking about the relationship and the other person) to minimum preoccupation (low relationship anxiety and where your focus is elsewhere and thinking minimally about the relationship, perhaps only when in front of that other person).

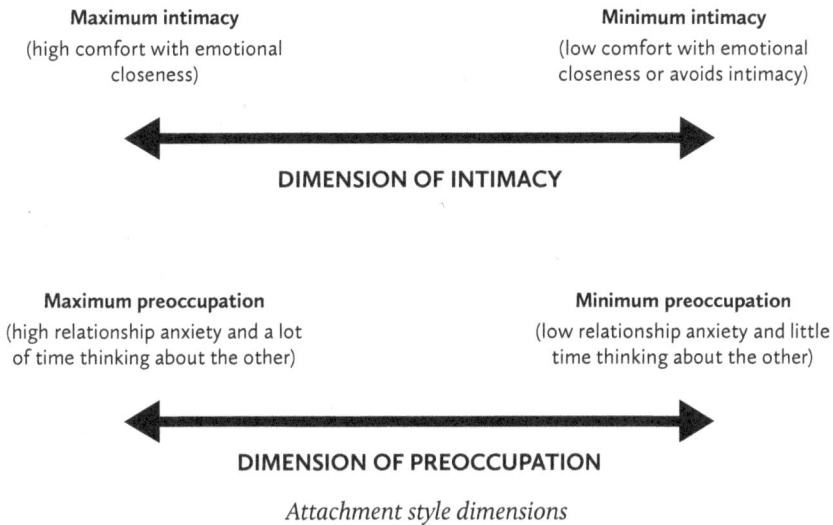

Maximum intimacy	Minimum intimacy
(high comfort with emotional closeness)	(low comfort with emotional closeness or avoids intimacy)

DIMENSION OF INTIMACY

Maximum preoccupation	Minimum preoccupation
(high relationship anxiety and a lot of time thinking about the other)	(low relationship anxiety and little time thinking about the other)

DIMENSION OF PREOCCUPATION

Attachment style dimensions

Secure attachment reflects a high comfort level of emotional closeness and intimacy paired with low relationship anxiety. Securely attached individuals are comfortable in the relationship, don't overly worry about their partner, are okay with spending time away from their partner and can focus on other areas of their life.

Anxious attachment reflects a high comfort level of emotional closeness and intimacy paired with high relationship anxiety. Anxiously attached people have a need for high emotional closeness and exhibit a high degree of anxiety, worry and focus about the relationship and their partner. Anxiously attached individuals turn towards the relationship to draw closer to the other when they need reassurance about the relationship.

Avoidant attachment reflects a low or avoidant level of emotional closeness and intimacy paired with low relationship anxiety. Avoidantly attached people hold little anxiety, worry or focus on their relationship or partner. They offer just enough to have some emotional closeness but withdraw if the other person gets too close or dependent on them. Avoidantly attached individuals turn away from the relationship to withdraw and distance from the other.

Disorganized attachment swings between both ends of the dimensions. people with this attachment style seek emotional closeness but also fear it and so withdraw to create emotional distance. This appears as switching between anxious and avoidant attachment styles, between turning towards and withdrawing from the other.

What is your attachment pattern?

Based on the descriptions of the four attachment styles and two dimensions, can you identify which attachment pattern best describes you? Perhaps identify where you would plot yourself on the two dimensions as a guide.

. . . .

. . . .

. . . .

When you experience conflict, rupture or worries in a relationship, do you turn towards or away from the other person?

. . . .

. . . .

. . . .

Do you seek and prefer emotional intimacy and closeness or emotional distance in relationships?

. . . .

. . . .

. . . .

What do you seek from others in relationships (e.g. support, reassurance, space)?

. . . .

. . . .

. . . .

What are your beliefs about relationships and how others will treat you or how relationships will end?

. . . .

. . . .

. . . .

Is there a pattern of behaviour in your relationships (e.g. seek closeness, withdraw)?

. . . .

. . . .

. . . .

Based upon what you believe your attachment style to be, there are ways to support you to develop a secure attachment style or reinforce it if you are already securely attached.

Developing a secure attachment style is to create a healthy balance and comfort in your relationships between emotional closeness and independence.

Ways to support a secure attachment style

- **Increase self-awareness:** Identify your attachment style and the repeated pattern it sets up in your relationships. Notice your feelings, beliefs and behaviours, especially when feeling triggered. Identify the source of your reactions and how they may represent your childhood or past relationships, as repeated in your present relationships.

- **Build self-esteem:** Work on strengthening your self-worth, self-confidence and self-esteem, to focus on yourself and build internal validation and not overly depend on external validation and reassurance. (See Chapter 13 to support this practice.)

- **Challenge negative beliefs:** Replace negative beliefs about your relationships with balanced views of what is possible within relationships and how to approach relationships. Try to catch negative thoughts as they arise to stop reacting and acting out because of these thoughts. (See Chapter 8 for how to challenge negative self-talk.)

- **Set healthy boundaries:** Setting healthy boundaries places you as an equal in relationships, as you communicate your needs and limits clearly, which communicates your self-worth and value. (See Chapter 22 for ways to implement healthy boundaries.)

- **Practise self-compassion:** Offering yourself self-compassion communicates in your self-relationship your own values and self-respect, and is reflected in your relationships with others. Self-compassion also offers you patience and gentleness as you work on your attachment style, make mistakes and grow through this journey. (See Chapter 14: Self-Compassion to develop this further.)

- **Practise emotional regulation:** Learn tools and techniques for emotional stability and robustness. Emotional regulation will support you to manage your emotions so that you are less triggered or emotionally reactive to threats, anxieties and conflicts in relationships. You learn to self-soothe as well as remain emotionally available to others without turning away or shutting down. (See Chapter 21 for emotional regulation tools and techniques.)

- **Practise open communication:** Start sharing your feelings, thoughts and needs in relationships respectfully and clearly. This supports realistic and communicated expectations to be met rather than unrealistic expectations that others will know what you need or how to respond to you, because you believe they 'ought' to know.

- **Build healthy relationships:** Be around those who offer healthy relationships consisting of secure attachment qualities – trust, empathy, respect, boundaries, emotional availability, consistency, clear communication, ability to talk through conflicts or ruptures. This offers you positive and reparative experiences of secure relationships, as a role model and framework for secure attachment experiences, for you to take forward into other relationships too.

- **Seek professional help:** Work with a therapist, who can facilitate your understanding and experience of your relationship blueprint and attachment pattern, and can support you to develop a secure attachment style and work through any underlying trauma or past experiences, which form your attachment style and move you towards healthier relationships and emotional robustness.

REFLECTIONS

How can you support yourself to develop secure attachment? What practices can you begin to implement?

. . . .

. . . .

. . . .

What steps or actions do you want to work on to support your development of secure attachment? What would you do? How might you do that?

. . . .

. . . .

. . . .

What are your reflections from this chapter?

. . . .

. . . .

. . . .

Are there any self-growth goals you want to set for yourself to support your development of secure attachment?

. . . .

. . . .

. . . .

How can these secure attachment practices be added to your self-care plan (see Chapter 4)?

. . . .

. . . .

. . . .

How can these practices and exercises further support your three relationship dimensions?

1. Relationship with Allah (swt):

. . . .

. . . .

2. Relationship with self:

. . . .

. . . .

3. Relationship with others:

. . . .

. . . .

CHAPTER 26

Emotional Availability and Emotional Intimacy

Emotional availability

Emotional availability is the cornerstone of emotional intimacy and healthy relationships.

Emotional availability is the capability and capacity to be emotionally open, present, engaged and responsive to emotional connections with other people. It is the capacity to connect with a breadth of emotions, to both share and receive emotions, to empathize with others' emotions and to understand and be understood. It is to be open to emotionally connecting with others and build relationships through investing time and energy in others and relationships, willing to be vulnerable and share your feelings and thoughts and to hold and honour other people's vulnerabilities respectfully. This builds a depth of emotional connection and bonds with others.

There can be challenges to being emotionally available with others if you experience emotional overwhelm or dysregulation, fear being vulnerable through feeling exposed and unguarded or risk of being hurt, carry unresolved emotional issues through past hurtful relationships or experiences, or struggle with emotional robustness to hold and contain your or others' emotions.

If you experience being emotionally unavailable at times in your life, you may wish to explore your beliefs, feelings, thoughts and experiences about relationships and being emotionally connected to others. Do you believe being emotionally close will lead to hurt, rejection, abandonment or pain? What do you believe about yourself receiving emotional connection and vulnerability from others? Explore what your beliefs are and where they originate from. Can you find reasons why they are true or untrue? Working through your barriers or difficulties for emotional availability with a therapist would be highly beneficial.

Practices to cultivate emotional availability

You can cultivate your emotional availability through these practices:

- **Develop self-awareness:** Connecting to and knowing your own emotions is the first step. Being emotionally available to yourself becomes the avenue to being emotionally available to others. Use self-reflection prompts or journaling to help you connect to yourself and your feelings. (See Chapter 17: Emotions to support you.)

- **Practise vulnerability:** Practise sharing your feelings with a trusted person. Start small by sharing something safe for you to speak about and how you felt about it. This could be a positive experience. It supports you to feel comfortable in sharing your feelings and experiencing someone being emotionally available to you, which then models how you can become emotionally available to them in return.

- **Use active listening:** Using active listening skills, holding the space and listening with full attention and no interruptions, being empathic, giving thoughtful and reflective responses and validating their feelings are ways of being an emotionally available 'container' to hold someone's emotional experience and to connect to what they are sharing and placing in your emotional 'container'.

- **Practise emotional regulation and robustness:** Learn to regulate your emotions to develop emotional robustness, as a solid 'container' for your and others' feelings. Being emotionally robust supports you to be able to be present and hold and support your and others' emotions. (See Chapter 20: Emotional Robustness and Chapter 21: Emotional Regulation for more.)

- **Set boundaries:** Practise putting boundaries around your emotional availability, so you manage and are in control of when you are emotionally available to others – that is, when your emotional container is 'open' for others to pour into you. This stops you from becoming overwhelmed or flooded with others' emotions. Instead, you hold a balance of when and what you are available for with others and when you need to be available for yourself. This supports the boundaries between self and others. (See Chapter 22: Boundaries for more support.)

Nurturing emotional availability takes intentional practice through building healthy and deeply connected relationships, but it greatly supports your wellbeing.

How can you support yourself to develop emotional availability?

. . . .

. . . .

. . . .

What steps, actions or practices do you want to work on to support your development of emotional availability? What would you do? How might you do that?

. . . .

. . . .

. . . .

Are there any self-growth goals you want to set for yourself to support your development of emotional availability?

. . . .

. . . .

. . . .

Emotional intimacy

Emotional intimacy is the deep emotional connection and closeness between you and another person. It derives from emotional availability and fosters trust, safety, acceptance, understanding, empathy, open communication and shared expressions of love and mutual support between you for secure, deep and meaningful bonds and relationships.

Emotional intimacy strengthens relationships to support your own wellbeing through better emotional health, sense of belonging, understanding of your experiences by being seen, heard and understood, and smoother repairs after ruptures or conflicts.

There can be challenges to emotional intimacy, like challenges to emotional availability, such as fear of being vulnerable, rejected or judged, carrying unresolved emotional issues that mean you find being vulnerable difficult, and lack of communication skills to be able to effectively share or express your feelings or to hear and hold others' feelings.

If you experience difficulties in being emotionally intimate, you may wish to explore your beliefs, feelings, thoughts and experiences about relationships and being emotionally intimate with others. Do you believe being emotionally intimate feels unsafe or will lead to hurt, rejection, abandonment or pain? What do you believe about yourself or what will happen if others are emotionally intimate and vulnerable with you? Explore what your beliefs are and where they originate from. Can you find reasons why they are true or untrue? Working through your barriers or difficulties for emotional intimacy with a therapist would be highly beneficial.

Practices to cultivate emotional intimacy

You can cultivate your emotional intimacy through these practices:

- **Open communication:** Share your feelings and thoughts. Listen back with empathy, non-judgement and compassion. Don't be scared to show your vulnerability, as it invites the other to mirror back with their vulnerability. What feels safe to share and with whom?

- **Emotional availability:** Practise emotional availability (as mentioned above). This helps to attune to others' feelings and respond to them appropriately, supporting them to feel seen, heard and understood by you.

- **Gratitude:** Share your appreciation of the other person to them. Express your thankfulness for their positive qualities and what they offer you in your relationship. (See Chapter 6: Gratitude to support this.)

- **Quality time:** Spend quality time together to enrich your emotional bonds and be in each other's presence. Spend time without distractions, engaging in meaningful conversation and activities to foster emotional depth. What fun activities can you do with your partner, family members or friends to spend quality time together?

- **Express needs:** Share your needs with others and hold space for others to share their needs with you. This supports open communication, trust and respect between you.

- **Shared goals:** Work together on a shared goal to foster a partnership and alignment with one another. This can be any goal, big or small, but one in which you both have a shared purpose and outcome.

- **Individual goals:** Support each other's goals and celebrate one another's achievements and successes, which fosters growth individually and between you. (See Chapter 16: Self-Growth on how to support your own goals and growth.)

- **Meaningful conversation:** Through open communication, speak on meaningful topics (e.g. feelings, thoughts, beliefs, values, goals, fears and hopes) to deepen and bring closer the intimacy between you. Set aside a specific time each day or week to have a dedicated space in your lives to share and come together. Ask questions such as 'What is the biggest worry for you right now?', 'What support do you need from me this week?', 'What goal are you working on?'

- **Conflict resolution:** Work together through conflicts, tensions or ruptures. Turn towards one another to resolve and do not turn away emotionally. Find solutions together and recognize the problem being solved together, instead of seeing each other as the problem itself. Practise forgiveness to move forward rather than hold grudges, and focus on working through the issue itself.

- **Relationship rituals:** Create and celebrate relationship rituals together, to foster shared memories and bonds over time and to feel valued and special in the relationship. These rituals are traditions, activities or habits that are meaningful to you, big or small. It could be a daily, weekly, monthly or annual tradition, such as a morning coffee routine, a weekly date night, a monthly day out or an annual anniversary celebration. Make it whatever feels appropriate for you, ensuring it is consistent, fun and meaningful. Adjust these rituals as and when necessary. What rituals do you already have in your relationships? What rituals would you like to create? What would feel fun and meaningful to you?

How can you support yourself to develop emotional intimacy?

. . . .

. . . .

. . . .

What steps, actions or practices do you want to work on, to support your development of emotional intimacy? What would you do? How might you do that?

. . . .

. . . .

. . . .

Are there any self-growth goals you want to set for yourself to support your development of emotional intimacy?

. . . .

. . . .

. . . .

Emotional intimacy and emotional availability are foundational to healthy relationships, as they build depth and closeness with others. They are not built quickly and require your patience and consistent practice, but they can create fulfilling relationships for you and nurture your wellbeing.

REFLECTIONS

What are your reflections from this chapter?

. . . .

. . . .

. . . .

How can these emotional availability and intimacy practices be added to your self-care plan (see Chapter 4)?

. . . .

. . . .

. . . .

How can these practices and exercises further support your three relationship dimensions?

1. Relationship with Allah (swt):

. . . .

. . . .

2. Relationship with self:

. . . .

. . . .

3. Relationship with others:

. . . .

. . . .

CHAPTER 27

Emotional Safety

What is emotional safety?

Emotional safety in relationships is the experience of feeling valued, secure and accepted in your relationships, with freedom to express your feelings, thoughts and needs, without receiving judgement or emotional harm. It is an essential element for all healthy relationships and nurtures your wellbeing.

Emotional safety is important as it supports you to be authentic, trusting and trustworthy, raises your self-awareness, reduces fears of abandonment or rejection, and creates the opportunity for resolutions and repairs after conflicts.

Emotional safety is built from core components of love, mercy, trust, open communication, acceptance, empathy, support, non-judgement and willingness to resolve conflicts and avoid emotional harm towards one another.

Emotionally safe relationships become a source of peace and safety. Through words and actions, honesty, openness, reliability and respect are demonstrated. Feelings, thoughts, fears and vulnerabilities can be shared with acceptance and empathy, without judgement, rejection or dismissal. There is an intentional avoidance of causing harm to others through ridicule, mocking, backbiting or abuse. Any ruptures or conflicts are worked through together, by each person turning towards the other, rather than blaming, holding grudges or turning away and avoiding each other or the problem. Emotional safety fosters a 'turning-towards' deeper connection between people.

Recognizing safe relationships

Recognizing the signs of safe or safe enough relationships, known commonly as green flags, is essential for identifying and understanding the quality and health of your relationships. When you can spot some green flags in your relationships, or recognize they need to be strengthened, you can nurture these to deepen your emotional safety and intimacy with others. When meeting new people, identifying green flags can also help you to recognize the potential to build healthy relationships.

GREEN FLAGS IN RELATIONSHIPS

- Open communication
- Active listening
- Non-judgemental attitude
- Consistent and reliable behaviour
- Words and behaviours match
- Takes responsibility and has accountability for themselves
- Gives and takes equally
- Values equality
- Trust
- Reliability
- Security
- Honesty
- Integrity
- Kindness
- Empathy
- Patience
- Understanding
- Openness
- Healthy boundaries
- Respect for boundaries
- Emotionally available
- Emotional support given to one another
- Comfort in sharing
- Expresses feelings and vulnerabilities
- Feeling heard, seen and understood
- Expressions of love, gratitude and appreciation
- Feels peaceful and safe enough
- Full acceptance of each other's authentic self
- Healthy conflict resolution
- Owns mistakes
- Supports during difficult times
- Supportive of family relationships and friendships
- Wanting to grow together
- Invests in relationship with time, energy and effort
- Support for self-growth and independence
- Celebrating each other's successes

Although this is not an exhaustive list, these integral green flags can support you to identify qualities for a solid foundation upon which to build, nurture and strengthen healthy relationships. Knowing that no one is perfect, and some green flags may be more obviously present than others, relationships with these green flags foster emotional safety and intimacy for sustainable, peaceful and fulfilling relationships and connections, which in turn support your wellbeing.

Reflecting on your closest relationships, which of these green flags are present and how do they show up?

. . . .

. . . .

. . . .

How do you feel emotionally safe/safe enough in your relationships? What do you need from yourself and others to feel this?

. . . .

. . . .

. . . .

What green flags might you need more of from others in your relationships? How might you nurture these?

. . . .

. . . .

. . . .

How do you show up as emotionally safe or safe enough for others? What green flags do you demonstrate?

. . . .

. . . .

. . . .

What green flags might you need to show more of, from yourself, in your relationships? How might you nurture these within yourself?

. . . .

· ·

· ·

What green flags might be a self-growth area for you to develop and strengthen?

· ·

· ·

· ·

Recognizing unsafe relationships

Equally, recognizing signs of emotionally unsafe relationships, commonly known as red flags, is essential for identifying and understanding the unsafe dynamics and lack of good quality and health in your relationships. In turn, this protects you and your wellbeing from the impact of red flags and unsafe relationships.

RED FLAGS IN RELATIONSHIPS

- Poor communication
- Inconsistent and unreliable behaviours
- Inconsistency between words and actions
- Only focused on self
- Lack of reciprocal effort or equality
- Lack of investment in relationship
- Lack of trust
- Lack of empathy
- Dishonest or deceptive
- Manipulative
- Uses guilt, gaslighting or confusion to control
- Judgemental, critical or condescending
- Self-righteous
- Doesn't acknowledge mistakes or weaknesses
- Passive-aggressive and defensive
- Plays the victim
- Constant drama, crisis or chaos
- Blames others and can't hold own responsibility

- Avoids issues
- Resentful and angry
- Emotional abuse
- Apologizes but with no change in behaviour
- Refuses to acknowledge or work on problems
- Stays stagnant in self-growth
- Lack of emotional availability
- Avoids emotional intimacy
- Dismisses or minimizes feelings, thoughts or opinions
- Withholds affection, love and support
- Conditional love or acceptance
- Demands trust and respect but doesn't give it
- Neglects others' needs
- Disrespects, disregards or violates boundaries
- Isolates others from their family or friends
- Selfish and wants others to themselves
- Envious or jealous of others' successes
- Overly dependent or enmeshed

If you notice any red flags in your relationships, it is important to understand them and their impact on you and others. It is challenging to build emotionally safe relationships with unsafe people, qualities and behaviours.

If you recognize any red flags in your closest relationships, it would be helpful to evaluate your relationships, how you can best support yourself and your wellbeing, and how to build green flags, and to identify if there is any risk of harm to you or others. You may wish to seek out professional support and/or therapy to explore your relationship dynamics and the impact on you, as well as any immediate or practical support you may need for your own emotional or physical safety.

Emotional safety is essential for healthy relationships, and recognizing red flags can support you to make positive changes and healthier choices in your relationships. Making intentional changes to your relationships, to move towards healthy dynamics and green flags, will support your wellbeing, identify which relationships are worth investing in or stepping back from, and help to build a healthy support circle for yourself (see Chapter 24 for further information on support circles).

Do you feel emotionally unsafe in your relationships? If so, how?

. . . .

. . . .

. . . .

What do you need from yourself and others to feel safer in your relationships? How might you nurture these?

. . . .

. . . .

. . . .

How might you show up as emotionally unsafe for others? What red flags might you demonstrate?

. . . .

. . . .

. . . .

How might you work on these red flags, to nurture more green flags from within yourself?

. . . .

. . . .

. . . .

What red flags might be a self-growth area for you to address?

. . . .

. . . .

. . . .

Cultivating emotional safety in relationships supports you to experience healthy relationships and support circles. It is an ongoing process of intentionally practising green flags and prioritizing emotional intimacy, emotional availability, emotional safety and emotional connection and vulnerability. It is a commitment to your relationships and others in your relationships. Pouring into healthy relationships also means pouring into your own wellbeing through intentionally nurturing fulfilling, peaceful and nourishing relationships.

REFLECTIONS

How can you support yourself to develop emotional safety in your relationships?

....
....
....

What steps, actions or practices do you want to work on to support your development of emotional safety? What would you do? How might you do that?

....
....
....

Are there any self-growth goals you want to set for yourself to support your development of emotional safety?

....
....
....

What are your reflections from this chapter?

....
....
....

How can these emotional safety practices be added to your self-care plan (see Chapter 4)?

....
....

. . . .

How can these practices and exercises further support your three relationship dimensions?

1. Relationship with Allah (swt):

. . . .

. . . .

2. Relationship with self:

. . . .

. . . .

3. Relationship with others:

. . . .

. . . .

CHAPTER 28

Therapy

A therapy journey

Engaging in a therapy journey is a positive step towards healthy relationships and balanced wellbeing. It is a path of self-growth and self-discovery. Understanding therapy, overcoming barriers and finding the right therapist for you can make a difference in your experience and outcomes.

The therapeutic process is one of exploration and discovery. There are no answers or advice given to you, but a process of discovery about yourself and the answers within you. This will support your emotional and relational development for the benefit of your wellbeing. You can learn about your emotions, understand your relationship blueprint and find ways to support healthy relationships with others and yourself.

Effective therapy is indicated by a good therapeutic relationship with your therapist, in which you feel safe enough, trust them and feel seen, heard and understood. The process is collaborative, whereby the two of you work together to explore and understand your experiences, with your therapist facilitating that process. The focus is on your self-growth and discovery, to support you to move forward with greater self-awareness, to inform your decisions and relationships in the future. Ultimately, good therapy values and works with you in your full identity and lived experience, taking into consideration all your identity characteristics, to offer you faith-sensitive and culturally sensitive therapy that meets your needs.

For Muslim clients, it is important for your faith beliefs and values to be acknowledged and respected, to be able to honour these within the therapeutic process and exploration. It is for your therapist to know the importance of exploring what faith means to you, its significance for you and how it informs your daily life, values and worldview.

For faith-sensitive therapists, it is important for them to be aware of key Islamic practices, principles and values such as prayer, gratitude, patience and compassion (as mentioned in this book), and how they inform how Muslim clients may view or approach their difficulties or challenges.

When faith is a central foundation of your identity and life, seeking a faith-sensitive therapist is essential, to allow your faith to be brought into the therapy room as part of your therapeutic process and self-discovery journey. This supports your healing and self-growth to be informed by and within your faith.

Myths about therapy

While we are seeing an increasing number of Muslim clients accessing therapy for their self-growth and wellbeing, there are still some cultural myths, stigmas or taboos surrounding therapy and mental health.

Some of these myths, stigmas and taboos include:

- Only people who are 'mentally ill' have mental health.
- Struggling with mental health means you have weak faith.
- If you're struggling, you just need to pray more.
- Going to counselling is a sign of weakness, weak faith or having a mental illness.
- Going to therapy is getting advice, an instant fix or selfish.

The truth is that struggling with emotional health, mental health or wellbeing does not mean mental illness. We all have mental health and wellbeing, and are on the mental health spectrum (from good health to ill health) and wellbeing spectrum (from poor wellbeing to balanced, optimal wellbeing). Struggling with mental/emotional health does not mean you are 'going mad' or there is something wrong with you. Everyone's mental/emotional health fluctuates up and down the mental health spectrum. Struggling with mental health is not a reflection of your faith or religiosity. Prayer can support your mental health, and speaking with a therapist or your GP and seeking professional help are additionally supportive for your mental/emotional health and wellbeing. Investing in yourself and your wellbeing is not selfish but plays an important role in being healthy for yourself and in all your relationships (with Allah (swt), yourself and others).

Accessing therapy

If you are considering accessing therapy here are some tips on choosing a therapist and going to therapy.

TIPS FOR ACCESSING THERAPY

- Identify what you want to work on in therapy. Is there a particular issue, area in your life or goal you want to explore?

- Identify your preferences for a therapist. Do they need to be a particular gender or faith? Do they need to be Muslim? Do they need to speak a particular language? Would you prefer a therapist who speaks in your first language? Do you want to access therapy in person or online?

- Identify what modality of therapy you want. Different modalities focus on different methods for exploration. Some are more structured and directive, which suits working with a specific goal or addressing cognitive changes in thoughts and behaviours (e.g. cognitive behavioural therapy (CBT), solution-focused therapy or eye movement desensitization and reprocessing (EMDR)). Other modalities are unstructured and emergent in their exploration, which would traditionally be called 'talking therapy' (e.g. psychodynamic person-centred therapy, humanistic) or creative therapies (e.g. art therapy).

- Look for a therapist who is qualified and registered with a professional body. Search for therapists listed in reputable counselling directories or a professional association directory. If you are looking for a Muslim therapist, search on the Muslim Counsellor and Psychotherapist Network (MCAPN) Counselling Directory (www.mcapn.co.uk) as all therapists listed are qualified and registered.

- Check qualifications and experience. When contacting therapists, ask about their qualifications and experience of working with the issues you are bringing to therapy.

- Specify faith-sensitive therapy. When looking for faith-sensitive therapy, ask therapists for their understanding of working with Muslim clients and how they offer faith-sensitive therapy to clients. Faith-sensitive therapists will know to explore your faith and ask how it informs your daily life and perspective on the issues you are bringing to therapy.

Making the most of therapy

Once in therapy, to make the most of your experience:

- **Check that it's a good fit:** Do you feel safe or safe enough with your therapist? Are you able to be open and vulnerable? Do you feel heard and understood? Are they empathic and non-judgemental? Are there established boundaries around the sessions? Is there a clearly written counselling contract that you have both agreed to? If you answer 'yes', it appears like a good fit. If you answer 'no' to any of these questions, you may wish to explore this with your therapist, as it may indicate a poor fit, lack of therapeutic relationship being offered by the therapist or poor boundaries.

- **Be patient:** Therapy is not a quick fix. The process can take time, and the learning and growth is not linear or straightforward. There will be steps forward and back, but always practise patience and self-compassion. The insights and self-discovery are worthwhile for your wellbeing and relationships.

- **Be open and honest:** Bring all of yourself into the therapy room. Growth comes from jumping into the process fully and being authentic about your experiences and issues, which will support your journey and learning.

- **Set goals:** Be clear and set specific goals for your therapy journey. Know what you want to work on and what the outlook may look like. This gives you a focus for your sessions and an overall direction of travel for your therapy journey.

- **Practise self-compassion:** Throughout your therapy journey, offer yourself consistent self-compassion, especially straight after your session when you may be feeling emotionally raw or vulnerable. Plan what you want to do after your session that would be compassionate or self-soothing (e.g. going for a walk, praying, journaling, grounding exercises or having a coffee).

- **Before sessions:** Reflect on any previous sessions and insights and identify what you want to bring to your session.

- **Post-session reflections:** After sessions, reflect on the session and what was explored. Use the following Post-therapy Reflections worksheet to support this practice.

POST-THERAPY REFLECTIONS

Ask yourself:

Were there any insights or discoveries made?

. . . .

. . . .

Identify any feelings, thoughts, reactions you noticed about yourself.

. . . .

. . . .

Note anything that stood out or was significant to you.

. . . .

. . . .

How did you feel in the session?

. . . .

. . . .

How was the session helpful?

. . . .

. . . .

Was there anything not mentioned that you meant to or needed to say? Why wasn't it?

. . . .

. . . .

What do you want to bring to your next session?

. . . .

. . . .

What do you need to reflect on during the week, before the next session?

. . . .

. . . .

. . . .

. . . .

Therapy can play an essential part in your wellbeing journey. Approach it with openness and authenticity. Finding the right therapist for you and investing in the therapeutic process will make a difference to your self-growth and relationships to support your balanced and optimal wellbeing.

REFLECTIONS

How might therapy support you?

. . . .

. . . .

. . . .

What self-growth areas or goals might you take to therapy for support?

. . . .

. . . .

. . . .

What preferences might you have for a therapist or type of therapy?

. . . .

. . . .

. . . .

What are your reflections from this chapter?

. . . .

. . . .

. . . .

How might therapy or professional support practices be added to your self-care plan (see Chapter 4)?

. . . .

. . . .

. . . .

How can these practices further support your three relationship dimensions?

1. Relationship with Allah (swt):

. . . .

. . . .

2. Relationship with self:

. . . .

. . . .

3. Relationship with others:

. . . .

. . . .

References

Hilali, Muhammad Taqi-ud-Din, and Muhammad Muhsin Khan. (1997) *Translation of the Meanings of the Holy Quran into the English Language*. Madinah: King Fahd Complex for the Printing of the Holy Quran.

Khan, M. (2020). Grow to Glow: The Art of Flowfilment. TEDx Talk. www.ted.com/talks/myira_khan_grow_to_glow_the_art_of_flowfilment

Khan, M. (2023) *Working Within Diversity: A Reflective Guide to Anti-Oppressive Practice in Counselling and Therapy*. London: Jessica Kingsley Publishers.

Levine, A., and Heller, R. (2010) *Attached: The New Science of Adult Attachment and How It Can Help You Find – and Keep – Love*. New York: TarcherPerigee.

Siegel, D. J. (1999) *The Developing Mind: How Relationships and the Brain Interact to Shape Who We Are*. New York: Guilford Press.

RAISING READERS

Books Build Bright Futures

Dear Reader,

We'd love your attention for one more page to tell you about the crisis in children's reading, and what we can all do.

Studies have shown that reading for fun is the **single biggest predictor of a child's future life chances** – more than family circumstance, parents' educational background or income. It improves academic results, mental health, wealth, communication skills, ambition and happiness.[1]

The number of children reading for fun is in rapid decline. Young people have a lot of competition for their time. In 2024, 1 in 10 children and young people in the UK aged 5 to 18 did not own a single book at home.[2]

Hachette works extensively with schools, libraries and literacy charities, but here are some ways we can all raise more readers:

- Reading to children for just 10 minutes a day makes a difference
- Don't give up if children aren't regular readers – there will be books for them!
- Visit bookshops and libraries to get recommendations
- Encourage them to listen to audiobooks
- Support school libraries
- Give books as gifts

There's a lot more information about how to encourage children to read on our website: **www.RaisingReaders.co.uk**

Thank you for reading.

hachette
UK

1   OECD, '21st-Century Readers: Developing Literacy Skills in a Digital World', 2021, https://www.oecd.org/en/publications/21st-century-readers_a83d84cb-en.html
2   National Literacy Trust, 'Book Ownership in 2024', November 2024, https://literacytrust.org.uk/research-services/research-reports/book-ownership-in-2024